PRAISE FOR OUR BELOVED FUTURES

~

"With rare and wild grace ~ this book has brought such strength and understanding to my heart. Its intelligence, and mythic, poetic beauty is breathtaking. Aubrey has written a poem, a prayer for the Earth and the New Dawn that sears the heart with the most beautiful and sure-footed golden initiation onto a pathway of peace, a blossoming pathway of Dawn. I recommend with all my heart! It is a powerful, golden lantern that shall light your way forward."

— ELEN ELENNA, AUTHOR OF *SILVER WHEEL: THE LOST TEACHINGS OF THE DEERSKIN BOOK*

"Aubrey Morgan Yee's book, *Our Beloved Futures*, is sown from the deep seeds of destiny and reaches toward a future we are brave enough to co-create. It moves through the grace of the venusian—visionary, sensuous, imaginal—and the precision of the solar—discerning, disciplined, sovereign. A luminous invocation where joy meets will, beauty meets leadership, and love becomes a strategy."

— RUTENDO L NGARA, AFRICAN INDIGENOUS KNOWLEDGE WISDOM KEEPER AND CO-FOUNDER OF ANCIENT WISDOM AFRICA/ANCIENT WISDOM FOUNDATION

"*Our Beloved Futures* is a heartfelt tribute to Gaia, the Earth Goddess! It is also a homage to Venus which has inspired Aubrey to present her wisdom to the world. This book will open your third eye, the eye of the heart. This is a timely book of ecological and spiritual significance for our planet."

— SATISH KUMAR, EDITOR EMERITUS, RESURGENCE & ECOLOGIST

OUR BELOVED FUTURES

AUBREY MORGAN YEE

Red Thread Publishing LLC. 2025

Write to **info@redthreadbooks.com** if you are interested in publishing with Red Thread Publishing. Learn more about publications or foreign rights acquisitions of our catalog of books: www.redthreadbooks.com

Paperback ISBN: 979-8-89294-039-9

Hardcover ISBN: 979-8-89294-056-6

Ebook ISBN: 979-8-89294-050-4

Audiobook: available on Audible

DEDICATION

To my family and friends, who are my communal body, loyal and patient, providing deep love and support, making my service to the world possible. To the more-than-human beings who persist and forgive despite our forgetting. To Hawai'i, the 'aina that has raised me and to whom I devote my life's work. To Earth, who waits patiently for our rising.

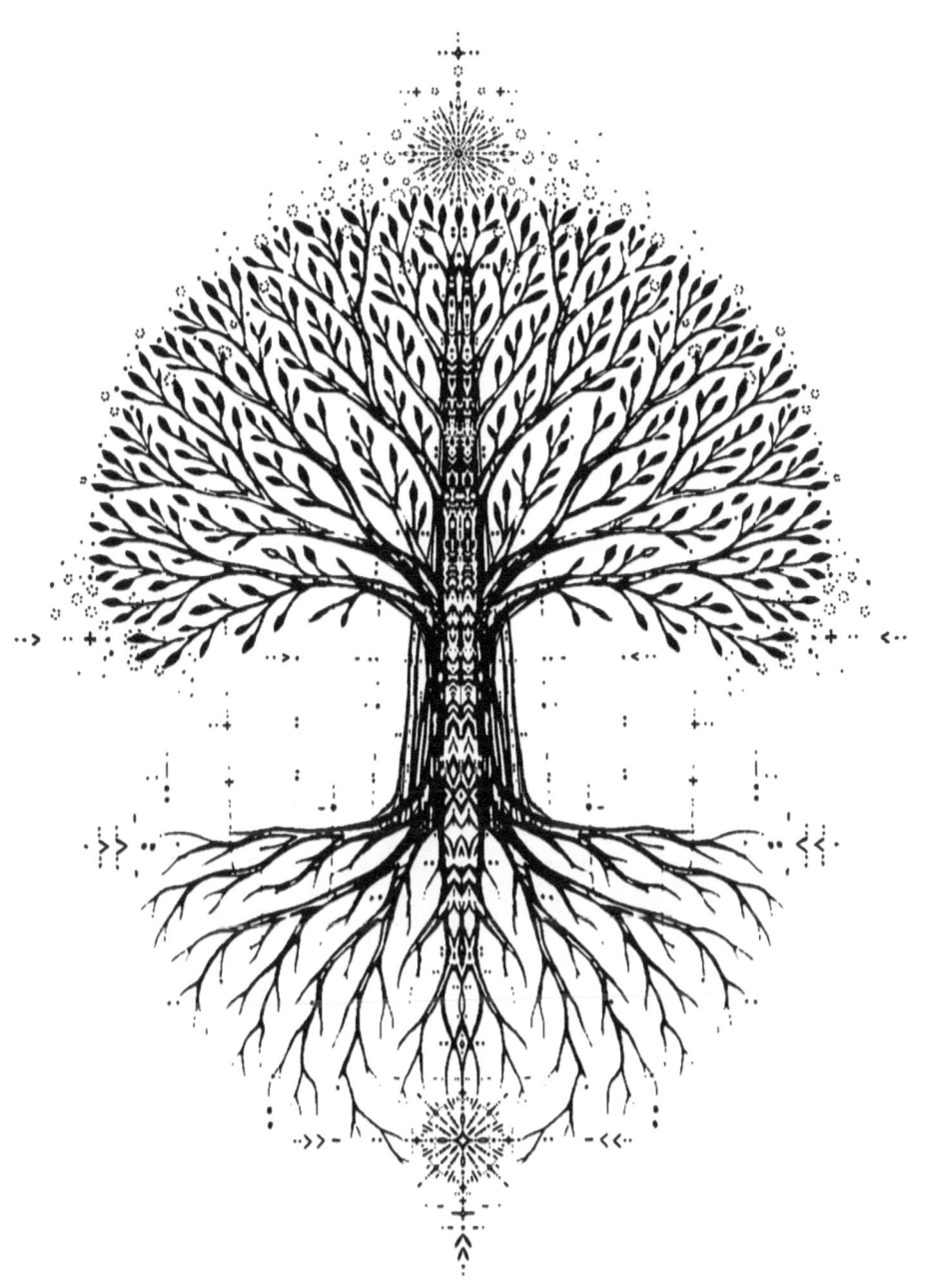

CONTENTS

PROLOGUE

HŌKŪAO, MORNING STAR RISING

The year is 2025. Year zero of the Great Turning. A year sages and elders are calling the Quaking. The splitting open of deep wounds that have been festering beneath a veneer of peace. I say *veneer* because this peace is only available to those who are lucky enough to be born in places characterized by a way of living that modern culture has labeled "progress." The rest of the humans and the more-than-human beings bear the brunt of an extractive and oppres-

sive source code of capitalism, colonialism, and empire that perpetu-
ates a fragile form of peace for some.

We are in the free fall of multi-system collapse. Polycrisis.
Metacrisis. Grasping for meaning as the world burns around us. From
the growing mountain of ash, this book rises as a message from the
ages. Both timeless and timely, it is woven through the tissues of my
embodiment. It is not mine, and yet it comes from me.

This book emerged first from a desire to aggregate and share my
poetry. Words and images that had passed through me to the page
across years of devotion to Earth, the animate, celestial goddess called
Gaia. Words and images hold dark spaces of grief enmeshed with a
persistent hope for humanity.

I started pulling from journals and scraps of memory, bringing the
poems and short bits of inspired thinking into one place. As I did this,
a channel opened. A portal of grace to divine wisdom that was both
mine and of the ancient futures.

My vessel has been prepared throughout my whole lifetime to
carry this forward to you. Many days, I wrote quickly without pause
in the early morning hours, and when I read back what was on the
page, I couldn't remember writing it. That's when I understood myself
as a vessel, steward, way-shower in humble service to something
beyond time.

I owe a great part of this book and my inspiration to the planet
Venus, a muse who has stewarded my own reawakening from an
ominous dark night of the soul.

The celestial dance of Venus around Earth matches the sacred
geometry of the flower of life, with a five-petaled rose in the center.
This sacred pattern is the visual image of her 584-day synodic cycle.
She moves from the evening star, seen at night, to a time when she
cannot be seen at all, which is representative of the underworld. She
then emerges again as the morning star. Her heliacal rise becomes
visible again in the early dawn hours. This dawning is a time of great
promise and potential, a powerful and positive omen. She moves fast
in the sky, painting the divine grace of this geometry.

The flowering of Venus mirrors the flowering cycles of our own descent from innocence, death, and rebirth as Earthlings. Ancient Mayan culture tracked her moves with intense precision and built huge temples to her grace. They understood the influence of this celestial being on our human bodies, made of water and minerals. The dance of Venus's flower of life holding keys to the secrets of creation, softly building worlds again and again. Inviting them to die with grace and then, with hope and promise, to be reborn anew.

I first communicated with Venus during her helical rise in the spring of 2020. As the world around me collapsed into a worldwide pandemic, my own internal world was similarly falling apart. Decades of hiding and numbing forced the death of the woman I had known.

Venus showed herself each night in the pre-dawn hours between the dangling roots of a sacred banyan tree that lives by the sea in Hawai'i, my home. As she rose, so bright, in the early morning hours, I found myself coming back into my wholeness, back to my innocence. Her twinkling light traveling across time and space was a salvation.

My love and connection with Venus grew stronger the next few years as my family was led to purchase land and build a permaculture farm and Earth Temple in Hawai'i called Hōkūao. Venus guided the whole process of this creation with power, source wisdom, and pure grace. The name Hokuao dropped into my consciousness while on a bike ride. A spirit-voice spoke the word *Hōkūao* with no context. When I got home, I looked this word up to discover that Hōkūao is the Hawaiian word for Venus when she becomes the morning star: Ancient Hawaiians revered Venus as Hōkūao, the farmer's star and an important navigational aid for voyaging from Tahiti to Hawai'i. They understood her celestial gifts as way-shower, leading us through the darkness and uncertainty to new lands, new futures. Magic and miracle.

Three nights ago, as I came to the end of this book's evolution, I woke at about 3 a.m. to a bright light shining in my bedroom window. So bright I thought it was either the moon or an airplane. My gut, my *na'au*, suddenly told me that light was Venus. The morning star had returned to light my way through this last phase of the work.

Venus, the planet of love and beauty, is also tied to the ancient

Sumerian myth of *Inanna*. In this myth, Inanna, a Sumerian goddess of love, beauty, and war, travels to the underworld to visit her sister Ereshkigal, goddess of the dead. As Inanna makes her way down to the underworld below the soil, she is stripped of her garments one by one until, fully naked, she is killed by Ereshkigal and hung by a hook for eternity.

Enki, the god of wisdom, intelligence, and magic, along with Inanna's loyal divine attendant Ninshubur, conspires for her release, promising Ereshkigal that Inanna will offer up another to take her place in the land of the dead.

Carried down through the ages of myth and legend, Inanna's descent into the underworld mirrors Venus's descent as the evening star. Stripped of all identity, Inanna must confront her own mortality in utter nakedness, no garments or jewels to hide behind. Inanna's time in the underworld mirrors the 50 days that Venus becomes invisible to those of us on Earth. The heliacal rise of Venus as the morning star is the mythical, metaphorical rise of Inanna, reborn through Enki and Ninshubur's gifts of wisdom, magic, and loyal devotion. But this rebirth requires a sacrifice; another must take her place. The other that she must leave in her place is the ego, the identity that once was and no longer serves. She must leave the self she once knew below ground, in the land of the dead, to rise again, reborn, innocent, holy, and whole.

We find ourselves now in the long dark of the underworld. Venus reminds us of our potential for rebirth. But the identity we have held so close as humans, individually and collectively, must be stripped away completely before we can be reborn. This is the Great Turning, spoken of by sages and passed through the ages. This is where we are.

I have spent many years studying and thinking about collapse. As a professional futurist, the image of the futures always spoke to me. I have understood for as long as I can remember that Gaia, our animate, emerald Earth, is being decimated by the systems created out of human fear, greed, and avarice. Systems of war and extraction are not native to our souls. These systems have been woven into us, and they can be purged, purified, and released. Beloved futures are possible.

Through my studies, I began to understand that collapse was already happening in many parts of the world and was coming quickly for those lucky enough to live in a borrowed denial. I also began to understand that death and rebirth are inescapable truths and that things must fall apart in order to be rebuilt, whole and holy in their innocence. We must fall apart. The world must fall apart. Our prayers are not for sustaining what we know must die. Our prayers are for a good death, a quiet and peaceful death.

The architecture of this book emerged as I gathered the words of poetry in my sacred basket. Alongside the collapse of civilizations, I have studied the human energy body. Knowing the truth of this extension of our biological form into frequency and energy, the reality of our chakras as portals to the infinite wisdom of an interconnected universe, I began to remember that the human energy body is our divine technology of redemption. It is our most native bridge to a graceful dying and a glorious rebirth.

I believe that through remembering how powerful and immense we actually are, we can collectively build worlds of peace, kindness, compassion, and synarchy with our beloved temple planet, Earth. She is waiting patiently for her children to return. We are ready for this aliveness. Peace on earth is possible. Our beloved futures are possible.

Worlds of what we call heaven already exist on Earth. This planet's inestimable beauty and abundance can hold all of us in grace. The energy body and chakra system is a rainbow bridge, a transition pathway from collapse to the new beginnings of the next world. We can face this with loving kindness and courage. We can release the fears of uncertainty and the unknown.

Part I of this book will take you on a journey through clear-eyed awareness of how bad things have become. Sacred witness of the mind-virus, the *wetiko*, that has infected our species. I use the metaphor of the butterfly to walk us through what it feels like for everything we have known to melt in order to emerge transformed. From the chrysalis to the dissolving within its casing, to the emergence as mariposa, the butterfly is a rebirth. Wet wings, wholly transformed.

You may have come to feel that the world is a violent, scary, sad place. That the problems are "out there" are to be solved by others, that they are growing and too numerous, and that you are not enough to do anything much. You may feel that numbing out or dissociation is the best survival tactic in a world gone mad. But we are each a fractal of the whole universe. When you find the courage to face the truth, you will discover the places where violence, fear, and greed have taken root within you. This is true for all of us enmeshed in modernity. This discovery can be painful. You are not alone.

You are so much more immense and powerful than your fear. In the frequencies of this book, you will remember that when you heal yourself in service to Earth and all her creations, you ripple the quantum effects of healing forward and back in time. Service to something greater than the small self is the key to magic and miracles. Collective liberation is our goal. None of us is free until all beings are free.

The grief of realizing how we have treated ourselves, each other, and the planet is an enormous grief. This book is here to hold that grief with you. I am here to hold that grief with you. We can be courageous together. Grieving is the first step to healing.

From the clear-eyed awareness of the moment we are in, Part II of this book will bring you to an understanding of your incredible energy body and how magical it is. You may not have even known it existed, or you may already work with this body of energy and light. Either way, may the frequency of the words in this book strengthen and brighten your energetic being, inviting a deeper and more centered you to emerge. One that has a tap root into Earth. One that can withstand the tsunamis of change that are washing over us and will continue for some time.

This book is both a journey and a portal. You can read it page by page or open to any page and see what wisdom wants to grace you this day. It's up to you how to engage with this mythopoetic becoming. You are entangled with this now. You are the morning star, co-dreaming our beloved futures with Earth as your ally. Each of us shines in this way.

As you read this book, allow the frequency of the words and the cadence of its message to wash over you. You don't need to understand it all with your linear, logical mind. A more ancient part of you will hear the call and become increasingly awake and aware as you read or listen to the words. This book works below the words on the page to bring you back to a self that has always been there, waiting for your permission to emerge.

Now is the time. All of you is needed here. We each come Earthside with a unique gift. Your gift is necessary and honored now. Allow yourself to face the painful truth of our moment. Allow yourself to melt and dissolve the parts of you that cling to the toxicity of the *world as it is* out of habit or fear. Allow yourself to rise up through the wisdom of the chakras in your energy body. Remember that you are the dreamer, awake, building beloved futures with Earth, immense in your powers of imagination. Allow yourself, like Inanna, to offer your ego to the underworld and thus be reborn. Wet wings. Holy. Morning star rising: Hōkūao. I see you. We are here.

OPENING PRAYER

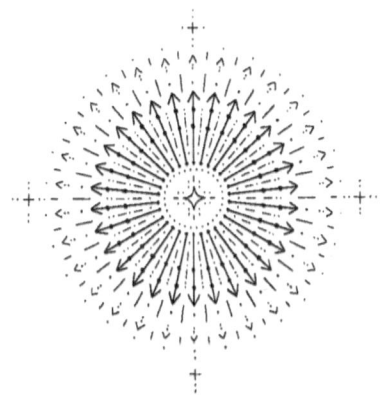

A prayer for the dying who live through these times of darkness. In honor of my sister, Heather, shocked from tiny, innocent embodiment to become my young ancestor. Her spirit and mine entwined in an ageless grace of aeons. This myth of ours holds a crack in the cement, the tender space for Life to emerge.

This is how it goes...
I wish to be messy
and awkward
with paint on my face and dirt under my nails...
The tattered dress I found at the thrift shop
takes the place of the tailored suit
that never fit right anyway.

When we remake the world, it won't be neat
And clean.
We will tear down the walls
Make messes of the kitchens,
build mud piles,
and sandcastles that get washed away
by the next big tide.
This is how it goes.
This is what I know.
In the desire to have the answers,
we kill the questions
before they have time to simmer and soak...
These are the times of unraveling
and only once the massive pile of thread is on the floor,
tangled in moss,
covered in muck
only then might we begin to see the pattern of light
that was always there,

waiting to be born.

SUPERNOVA

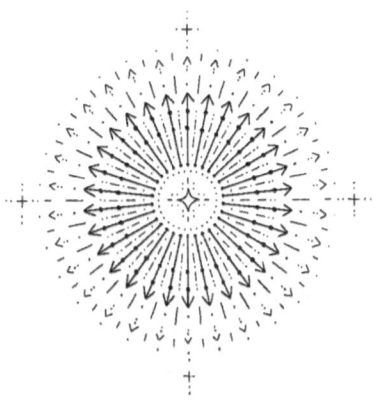

What do we do at the edge of the world, when time has stopped and truth hibernates with bear in her cave? We gather the buffalo hide and clear space for the moon's lodge. We remember the dreaming power of human and more-than-human entanglements. We set a place for intuition and inspiration at the feast of imagining.

As we begin this journey together, I invoke a mythos for the new beginnings, for the seeds with wings, for the brave ones who came to dance–to witness the supernova of humanity, flourishing in fluorescence.

The Age of Consequence

I honor your gods
To journey beyond the old limits
Of all that has become wearisome
This is the age of consequence.
We bathe in the dying,
Allowing our skins to compost back to Gaia.
The dying is the moment.
Where is joy in this suffering?
Where is the radical choosing of simplicity and
fasting in
the feasting?
To see the bounty and digest its illusion.

To transmute the gold back into its original sweat and
blood
Until dirt becomes the sacred sovereign.
What is this turning? Why have we come?
White bodied and dis-identified,
A soul that never fully understood its skin
Learning gratitude for the form of this lifetime.
The artifacts of neoliberalism
Alive on a shelf of remembering.
They will be passed on as the cautionary tale.
The one in which we forgot the ways.
On the days when remembering
Is as nectar is birdsong
And tobacco clears air with its sweetness.
The undoing complete.

The restructuring eternal...

Queer beings speak in seeds
as flowers fall from their lips.
I am surrendered.
My hand to your heart is this radical act.
Touching wound to wound, we become.
I am Aubrey
A queen of the Elven ones.
Ancient teacher with wisdom codes of a spiritualized
    and intergalactic Earthworld
Stored within my bones and my blood.
I speak with the elemental realms,
Weaving their wisdom songs of earth and stars
Into human languages.

When I see myself in this,
I can sing my breath.
I am Fae folk.
I am found.

MYTH-MAKING

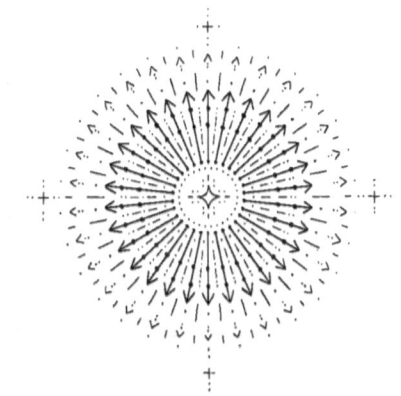

A myth is, at its root, a story to help us remember how to live in right relations with life. Myths have accompanied humanity since our dawn as Earth beings. In song, spoken tales, written stories, music, and movement, myths have been ways of weaving dreams with flesh. And at this time of the Great Turning, the years that will shape us, the transitions that will break us, the fires that will provide the ash from which to gather, now is a time for new myths. These myths are the ones that invite and nurture new futures of peace and blooming. The ones that hospice old ways of pain and suffering.

Naming is a powerful myth-making exercise that we perform and resurrect daily. The name for a thing guides and contains our experience of it. Our own name is a myth. One that we carry through our lifetime. I believe that our souls choose our names between lifetimes to guide the learning in each particular embodied experience. That belief is my myth, maybe it is yours too.

Perhaps this sacred name was honored. The whisper of your name, heard by your chosen parents, and spoken at your birth. The resonance of ages imprinting on the energy body, starting a spiral of life experiences emanating from the mythos. Perhaps, the sacred naming was whispered to your parents, and doubt crept in. Whispered wind was illegible, ego chose otherwise, and the name became something else. Out of place, out of your timeline. You may have always felt that the name you were given was somehow not yours. Trust this, too.

The name you dreamed in the bardos between lives remains alive in the wind. It travels with you in the ether. It speaks to you in your dreams. You can still catch it and sing its vibration into your soul field. This, too, is part of the journey you chose when you chose your parents. Knowing that forgetting and remembering, learning to trust your own whisper, would be part of building the strength you need in this lifetime. Finding your true name is like a song being sung through you. The rightness is pure; it is simply there. Renaming can be a potent and powerful act of soul retrieval.

You're allowed to feel your true name and how it calls you. The Earth will speak this name to you, and you will know it is yours because your soul will feel it is home, seen, known.

When held with reverence, our names inform, inspire, and remind us of our purpose, what is ours to do during this particular incarnation. The myth of your name holds power and potency. Be curious and willing to receive it. It is a code of your remembrance.

I am Aubrey. A name given at my birth that means *queen of the elven ones*, the shining ones, the Sidhe (pronounced "shee") of Celtic legend. The Aos Sidhe are the ancient fairy folk of Ireland, my ancestors, star beings who came to Earth to be devotees of Gaia. Gaia, the celestial goddess who *is* the planet Earth. She is a sentient being on her own path of growth and awakening. I am devoted to her. I am Aos Sidhe.

When I remembered this name that I chose, Aubrey, my lifetime of confusion and hiding suddenly made sense. As Fae, Aos Sidhe, one of the ancient earth tenders, it makes sense that I feel the pain of Gaia's suffering. It makes sense that being human has been so shocking during a time of darkness and violence within the dominant cultures. It makes sense that I feel most at home in the waters and forests of Gaia's grace. *I* suddenly make sense when I remember my name.

I choose to believe the myth of my names. Learning to live into them. I had forgotten this innocence for many years. I suffered in self-sustained darkness, alone and silent to myself. The protections around my heart, a solid wall of impermeable suffering. I had forgotten my essence in a cloudy veil of not-enoughness.

Believing myself to be unlovable, I was, therefore, unsafe to be fully seen. I know now that this was protection from the shock of arriving in a world gone mad, where violence reigns and the Earth is under constant attack. Once I was able to see, really see, the absurdity of freeways, the ridiculousness of marketing, the hard work of perpetuating daily micro and macro violences, only then was I able to let down these guards and relax the walls around my heart.

I could see that we, as a collective of humans, are powerful beyond measure in our dreaming of the world. We just distorted our dreams into nightmares. We built massive dams to stop rivers from flowing so we can power homes, where we sit depressed and devoid of our connection to the waters in that same river, and her fish.

We build huge buildings with unimaginable capacities for housing each other, but never meet our neighbors and live in alienation from each other. We create chemical foods to feed a world that has forgotten the inestimable magic of a fruit growing quietly and peacefully on a tree.

We are powerful beyond measure, and when this power of divine design is placed back in loving service to Gaia's dream, when we remember how to listen to her whispers and speak in her metaphors, when we once again trust life, a potent and lasting florescence will be released on this temple planet once again. The flowering of humanity is possible. Peace on Earth is possible.

This book is the tale of that re-member-ing of myself, of yourself, of ourself. This is a tale of relighting the energetic centers at the core of our human design

The centers that pulse and pull energies of love into our embodiments, animating us with joy and peace. We were literally made for this. Our human design is a portal of energetic and frequency medicine that most naturally knows how to perpetuate peace. Everything else is a distortion of our design. This peacefulness is the truth of who we are as humans.

Peace is not a state of perpetual happiness. Peace is a vibration of acceptance of what is. A peacefulness with what is. And the wisdom of not knowing the future. We are peaceful with that, too.

This book will take you on a journey through the human energetic system, known as the chakra system. Each chakra is a portal that pulls energy in from the universe to power up our human biological bodies. Each chakra represents an aspect of ourselves. When we fully activate the potential of these energy centers in our biological design, we activate the full potential of what it means to be human.

We have been operating for the most part without the conscious knowledge of and engagement with this energetic system of ours. Coming fully online and into our aliveness as a species is the opportunity of this moment on Earth. It is the alternative to our extinction.

We are all of epic origins, epic proportions. Love only works that way. Dream again into the myth of you. It is your divine design. I have come to tell the tale of my soul that came to Earth by way of the Betelgeuse supernova. A blast of star explosion, lighting our destiny as Earth-tenders. A supernova yet to be witnessed on Earth, its light still making its way here while our souls tend to the Great Turning. Our sister, Gaia, calling for us to arrive during this time. To awaken and remember.

The supernova was our gateway to reentering Earth with the

ancient ways of the Sidhe to guide us. Pathways of star ancestors guiding from within. As humanity opens its eyes from deep, fearful slumber and becomes again with Earth, we find each other, and we remember together. Gaia's abundance becomes, again, a fantastic blooming. A riot of color and love. Witnessed as glory by Earth angels and all the cosmos. This myth, this one, makes sense of my life.

What is the myth of your name? The myth your soul chose to curate your life's path. Find the myth of your life and live it with abandon. Make meaning in *story,* and you will find yourself. You will find your purpose. These are the stepping stones to joy.

In the midst of suffering and the carnival of human creation, when you walk this path, just one step at a time, you will find peace. My myth is woven with the myth of Earth. All myths are. They speak her song to help us remember our unique dance. There is only one dance like ours in all the cosmos.

I have come earthside by way of a cloud to bring threads of golden light to the trees of a new dawn. I can see this vision in my mind. The sparkle of star leaf and the rhythm of tree whispers. I am remembering hers, the wisdom of the wind, the depth of the waters, and whale songs. I am yours, too. We are woven. We are, and always have been, of the same wisps of cloud.

Like tendrils of light and roots, we braid the subterranean realms of soil's rich humus to surface new life in Earth's majestic realms. She has brought us here with her magnetic love. What we call gravity is the unconditional love of her embrace. We are experiencing this now as *human becomings,* on the way to herald something even we have not yet seen. And in this remembering, in this passage, we sing songs of peace.

It is the light and the step-stone–peace. For that is our truest essence–peace. Everything else is from a different vibration. A vibration of forgetting. Those heavy energies of violence and fear, the opaque ones, are merely lights that forgot how to shine. They offer the gift of contrast that allows us to understand the spectrum of experience. Not to be confused with our natural ways of being, they are there to give us the chance to love even more.

Where in my heart am I still not free? The dark and light play with one another, intertwining like the banyan tree, encompassing *all that is* with a choking embrace. I once sat with a banyan tree on the edge of the sea for many moons, watching a star sparkle and speak to me. I had yet to learn that she was Venus, my relative, my guide. I was in the darkest night of my soul, drowning in fear, in an attempt to hide from feeling. I was weak and scared, and love saved me. The banyan saved me. Venus saved me. I saved me.

Feeling is a courageous act. I am here now to tell you that we can feel. That we are meant to feel. That we can practice our way into feeling fully, and that on the other side of that courage is profound joy and deeply abiding peace. That grief is only possible when you love so much. That love is our purpose.

Some days I am unsure and off-balance. I don't know how to find the center once more. This is where forgiveness lives. Teetering front to back, finding the center line, finding balance. In a small earthen hut with a soft grass roof, my soul can rest in the dirt and smell earth again. The distance between there and this human life is my destiny.

There are some who came earthside to restore balance with Gaia. You were magnetized to this reading because you remember this. We bring the unconditional love that knows this true essence and forgives all. You came here with me. You remember this, too.

How long have you been hiding your wings? It is time now to allow their gossamer shimmer to unfurl in delicious fullness. Allow their weightless loving to beat softly again. It is safe, dear one. You are safe and you are seen. I bow to your beauty. We are here.

I trust the wisdom of plants
Tender shoots rising to sunlight
Trusting their reach on a language of heat
And alchemy
Patient as a tree
Who can see the boy
Tangled in her leaves
Who lets his love
Pull her nutrients into branches
I trust the wisdom of plants
Who give me their most precious parts

Life-giving sacrifice
With no expectations of return
The sweetness
Enough for both of us

I trust the wisdom of plants
And the whispers of wind
The waters of land and memory
Passing between us
In a fluid beauty
That cracks my heart in 1,000 ways

I trust these wisdoms of plants
The ones who persist

Who offer their flesh
Who flower in forgiveness

I trust the wisdom of plants
The ones who never left
Their song in the seed

Speaking soft poetries of Life

May I always be in right relation. Never righteous, always wholesome. Whole and Holy. Divinely on purpose. Divinely on time.

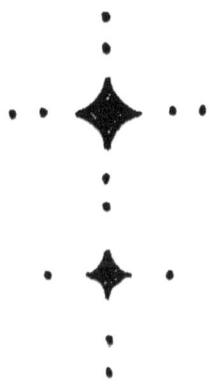

I bear witness to the turning of ages
The times sages spoke of...
We enter the sacred drift once more
Between worlds
Tethered only to our love...
Guided by our grief
We cry in the knowing of what can be
We cry in the grief of what we have done
It is our deepest work to forgive.

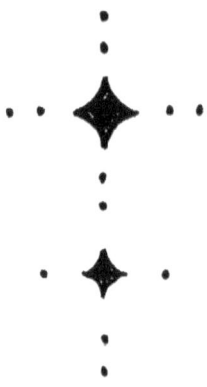

In my dreamspace one night, a circle of banyans arose from the ash of yesterday. The banyan's tangled branches held open mycelial remembering of ancient tomorrows, lit by the hum of ancestors. As their roots rose out of dark earth soil, a space was made within their center. As if a transparent temple of crystalline grace held a vibration to open the roots in tangled shapes of wisdom. I had glimpsed Venus earlier that night between the branches of a banyan, earthside by the sea. I knew these trees were connected.

Tree of life, tree of wisdom, tree of futures past, returning to Earth as portent of the coming. Leaves ablaze with Earth's dream, the banyan reminded me of the forever woven grace of peace. This tree holds within its life force the codes to gently wake us all from the imprisoned nightmare of our own making. Like a mother kisses her daughter to wake, the banyan holding grace at her core. The one that would remind us of the rhizomatic language of soil and salt.

Teaching us the ancient ways to be with Earth as the inestimable being that she is. The one that would guide us from our fugitive state, refugees of violence, to the connection and joy of our natural peace ways. Guiding us down the pathways to being again as innocent as bird, whale, and tree, herself.

In the dream, I entered the temple of roots and found soft flames of crystal, color, and light. Each one burning the ways back to balance. Step by step, I absorbed and digested their knowings. Step by step, I remembered my immutable ancestors, the Sidhe, the shining ones. The fae folk who taught my life's song, who wished me well when I decided to journey to Earth. From within the temple, words dripped like sweet waters of life force, eros, Love. This book is my temple of devotion. It is the temple of Venus and the banyans. It is dedicated to you.

And so we begin. The circle is open.
The banyan holds our love. Welcome.

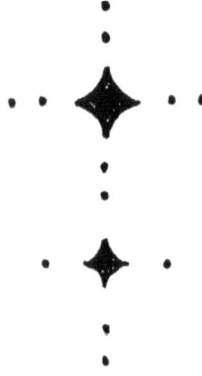

PART I

METAMORPHOSIS

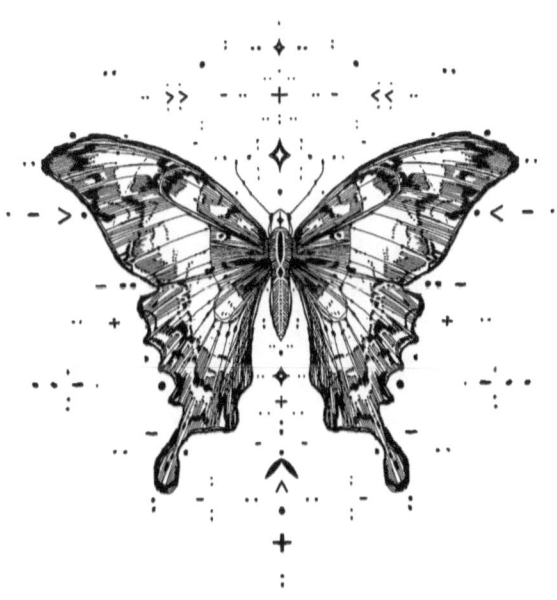

1

MYTHOS FOR NEW BEGINNINGS

THE RAINBOW BRIDGE

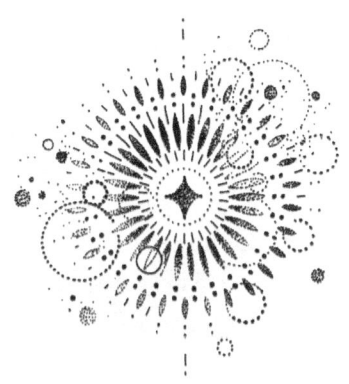

This is a tale of what comes after. After we remember our true nature as peace. We have enough tales about how things fall apart. This is the tale of the braid of love and truth that held together long enough for our traveling, as everything around it frayed and then unraveled without ceremony. Like the roots of the banyan that come from its branches above, slowly walking a pathless path, one root tendril at a time, it was all too slow for human perception to understand this revolution in its fullness. We couldn't see the totality until the revolution became irresistible and the takeover complete. Until roots outnumbered stones and entanglements became like breathing. The temple, still visible beneath the roots, creating new worlds, offering generous cracks and fissures within which to imagine again. In the space between, that blessed space that the crack holds open, light can emerge, and something truly new may be birthed. This is the story of that secret.

The secret has always been in our divine design—the truth of us, hidden in plain sight. By the time of the Great Turning, the sight necessary for seeing this truth had become a forgotten memory for most. For those who came to remember us back to peace and who were meant to teach the remembering to the others, the secret was as natural as a heart beating. They saw clearly the mycelial tendrils of connections, the weavings that always are, and they told us how to remember that our human bodies are a rainbow bridge of incredibly powerful energy centers. These centers both root us to the Earth, our mother, and connect us upwards to the celestial heavens, our original home. We, the humans, are the bridge between celestial wisdom and Earth's memory.

Chakra is an ancient Sanskrit word for wheel or circle. This word is just one way to name the etheric body, the whirling energy centers that pull information from the universal realm into physical form to be experienced on Earth's plane. These centers translate source information into form through patterns of sacred geometry. Everything we experience and know in physical form is made this way. It is all energy and frequency made into form through the geometry of Love that is sacred and eternal. We are Love made into form through energy and frequency. That is the truth of you.

When a baby is forming in the womb, the energy body forms first. A result of the thoughts, frequencies, and vibrations of the mother and her environment. On this body of energy and aether–the life force that connects all things–biology attaches tissue and cells to create shapes through the patterning of sacred geometry. We are, from the beginning, beings of magic and miracle. When we remember this, we will treat the sacred portals of sexuality, conception, and birth with pure reverence. Each of us is an expression of god, light, source, being made into sacred form and function for a finite lifetime of human experience. We are inestimable and magnificent.

Our entire universe is a pulsation of light and frequency, and our chakras are the sacred technology that pulls that pulsation from formlessness into form through the assembly of sacred geometric patterns using biology as its substrate of creation. The light body is our first body. It is always with us. There are tales, both ancient and new, of beings who attained such a heightened state of awareness and incarnation that they reactivated their rainbow light body–their full energetic system coming online at the moment of transition to what we call death.

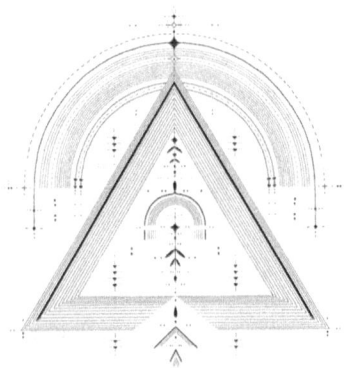

This being human is a rainbow bridge,
connecting heaven and Earth.

Anuenue is the Hawaiian goddess of the rainbow. As we stand on the quicksand of the age of consequence, a rainbow circles Earth. Hawaiians know that Anuenue connects us from Earth to the realms of the divine. Portending grace or the storm. Which way shall we turn? Grace or the storm? We begin by remembering that we have a choice.

The prophecies are everywhere.

There are tales of the prophetic rainbow warriors. Believed to come to earth at a time of great destruction. A group of peoples from a rainbow of skin colors and nations, this prophecy is shared by many native American peoples.

The Shambhala warrior prophecy has been carried on breath by sages deep in the mountains of Nepal, Tibet, and Ladakh. According to this prophecy recorded 12 centuries ago in the Kalachakra Tantra, there will come a time when the world is on the brink of annihilation. A time when all hope is almost lost. When a group of barbarian powers has plunged the Earth into darkness with technologies of total destruction and annihilation. A collective of Shambhala warriors, warriors of peace, will be activated. This is a group that has no outward similarity and no uniform or central authority. Led by the authority of Love, with compassion and interbeing as their tools of peace, their weapons of Love, they will go into the halls of the barbarian powers to stop the weapons of destruction and bring about a golden age. This is you. *You* have come.

Crazy Horse, a Lakota Sioux wisdom elder, is said to have prophesied days before his death: "I see a time of seven generations when all the colors of mankind will gather under the sacred Tree of Life and the whole Earth will become one circle again."

The rainbow reminds us of our sacred light body. The rainbow light of Anuenue is brought to us by the Sun through the wisdom of water falling as rain. She has come to remind us that the secret was always within our divine design. The seven chakras are our soul's essence that constitute the light, the etheric body upon which our physical body is built. These chakras are the color of the rainbow. The rainbow warriors, the Shambhala warriors, the peaceful warriors are all of us. All of us, when our body of light is activated, and we become Love once again.

This is ancient wisdom, woven through cultures, peoples, and understandings. Whatever words we use to describe it, it is a human truth. It is a key to our becoming fully human as we were designed. It is why you are here now. It is why I am with you. It is what has been distorted to uphold the exhausting systems of violence and oppression we see and experience now. The toxicity, distraction, fear frequencies, regrets, and shame that populate our dominant culture are blocking our profound human design from realizing the miracle that we already are and have always been.

Once we have fully formed in our biological bodies, these whirling chakra centers pull in source information as energy and process this information through the organs of our hearts and minds, and through the collective consciousness of the millions of beings, bacterial and viral, that inhabit our bodies. We are always so much *more than human* in our humanity.

This book invites you to travel the rainbow bridge of your energy body. You are a bridge from heaven, the celestial star home of our ancestors, to Earth. And as we begin, once again, to consciously connect with the etheric body, we must come to terms with the age of consequence, the Great Turning, the polycrisis and meta-crisis. We must face the grief of what we have done. We must forgive ourselves and become wholly human. We must collectively practice ways to digest and compost the profound darkness of this moment in time for the human and more-than-human-species on Earth, for Earth herself.

You may live in relative peace and wonder where this darkness is when you have enough food to eat, a house to live in, a family that loves you, a healthy body, and a safe place to live, learn, and love. And yet, despite that place of privilege, you feel inner unrest. Voices and emotions that keep you from the true, deep peace that is your birthright. For all but a few humans alive today, the shallow, superficial experience of privileged peace is only possible because of the immense suffering of others. The safety enjoyed by some is secured by the horrific oppression of multitudes of others, human and more-than-human.

The products consumed by a select few are created by extraction, waste, and slavery or near-slavery conditions. The health enjoyed by some bodies that have access to clean food, water, air, and adequate health care is dependent on and secured by war, violence, and the torture of multitudes of others. These pockets of peace are not true, deep, or authentic. They are fragile, delusional, and fleeting. The work we do here, together with these words and this book, is about a lasting, deep, unshakable peace. This book is about peace for all beings on Earth.

Peace on Earth is possible.

The unfathomable nature of that simple statement reminds us how far we have come from true peace.

The prophecy of the caterpillar guides our journey into understanding our paradox and the ways out and through. The caterpillar begins its life as the ultimate consumer. Caterpillars eat their way through as many leaves as they can, as quickly as possible, growing in size and getting fatter, fatter, fatter, without stopping. Until one day, something shifts. They realize they can eat no more. Their bodies freeze into a strange shape, signaling their next phase of transformation. They build a wall of skin around themselves until they are fully encased, sealing the chrysalis of skin with a thin seal of gold. And then, they begin to dissolve, melting until no form of their previous being is left. They literally become a formless goo.

As they turn to goo, cells within their being that were previously dormant awaken. These are called *imaginal* cells. Imaginal cells contain the blueprint for the new form or structure that has always been there, waiting to emerge. Until this moment of melting into goo, these imaginal cells have existed in isolation, as single-celled organisms, thinking they were all alone, not understanding their purpose, wondering why they existed at all. As they awaken and realize the moment of metamorphosis is dawning, the imaginal cells remember their blueprint, their reason for being, their shared purpose, and their collective liberatory destiny.

At first, the caterpillar cells attack the imaginal cells, thinking they are foreign invaders. But the imaginal cells are immune to this attack, and they persist, rooted in their purpose. Eventually, as they join and remember themselves, they inform the new shape that was always waiting to be born from the etheric memory. These seeds of future potential find each other and begin to speak the alchemy of profound transformation. Together, they build the body of the butterfly, a profoundly different form from the caterpillar, until finally, this new being is ready to emerge, wet wings drying in the wind. The caterpillar that once only knew consumption is now ready to fly, a pollinator who creates and sustains *Life*. Mariposa. Papillon. Lelelele. Butterfly.

Our pathway to peace is this very process.

Find the others. Find the imaginal ones who dream the big dreams and love them fiercely.

Dissolve empires within and without. Start with the memory of your cells and work outwards to the memory of your culture. Dissolve the desire for *power over* and remember the true nature of your being as peace.

By exploring the dissolution of empires, the chrysalis, a time of becoming goo, we begin to understand how deeply the mind-viruses of consumption, extraction, separation, and violence have woven their way into every cell of our bodies, minds, and cultures.

As we imagine the mariposa, the butterfly already emerging through us, we can wake from the nightmare that we dreamed unconsciously. We can forgive ourselves for our sleep. We built this world. We can build others. Worlds where our peace increases the peace of others. Where our joy is built on the lasting joy and health of all beings on Earth and Earth herself. This is *possible*. This *is* possible.

The mind was always meant to be the seat of imagination that translated the visions of Earth and sky through our bodies into Earth form. But the mind is a trickster and easily imbalanced. Once we listened only to the mind and the frequencies of fear, doubt, and scarcity, we lost fluency with the languages of Earth and sky. This is what we know as *the fall*. This is what we experience as off-balance and unnatural ways of violence and fear.

Our remembering is simple. Not easy, but simple. When operating in coherence with our divine design, humans are doulas to life. We midwife new realities with Gaia, our temple planet, the goddess of

Earth, as the dreamers of her dreams. We do this easily, joyfully, and simply when we remember who we are.

We are a tribe called *human*. Rising from Earth to greet the sun. Lying down at the end of the day to greet the moon in our dreams. Simple beings of Earth. Earthlings of soil and water. We sing as birds and swim as fish. These are lives of magic and reverence, held by a mother who loves us unconditionally.

All over the world, we are assembling.
All over the world, we are finding our kind and building the new Earth
beneath the tatters of the old.

One day, we will shake the last vestige of ash and drink again of clean waters, fresh air, clean food, and loving relations. Not just a select few, but everyone. The lie of scarcity holds us hostage to beliefs that don't speak in Earth's native language. When we become legible again to our destiny as Earthlings, we will know that peace is our vibration.

Love washes over hate and brings us back to our source as light. We drop the knife of modernity that has cut us over and over and over again. We finally release, let go, surrender, trusting that there is something more. Trusting that we will be safe, that we were always already saved. And when we drop that knife, we release pure light in its place. And that light, it goes everywhere.

2

CHRYSALIS

WAKING FROM THE NIGHTMARE

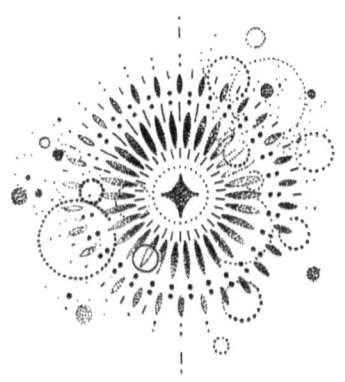

The planet, her people, and all of her creatures are exhausted. This is the time for rest and regeneration. We are melting into goo. We are like the caterpillar that crawled into her cocoon and melted into formless goo; from mindlessness and distraction back into our innocence. In our emerging, beloved futures, we will hold wholesome space for the possible and allow ourselves to sip from the soft, regenerating waters of creativity again.

Anxiety, fear, regret; these are hungry ghosts often moving at night. I woke last night to gut-wrenching anxiety. It gripped and held me at my core. Confused about its source, I felt my mind kick into gear. The mind is always seeking to control, protect, define, and capture meaning. My mind immediately went to work, attempting to "make sense" of it, this fear. To attach meaning to anxiety's arrival. *It must be that person, that email, that scarcity, that change that is coming. That's what this feeling is.*

My mind raced to find a story to attach to the anxious feeling, to build it a home in my being, to invite it in and define it. In a flash of pure insight, I knew that anxiety was not mine. The anxiety had a life of its own; it was outside of me, trying to get in.

This animal, this beast, it travels. It travels from person to person, often when the world is most quiet, because then it can awaken our mind and ask it to find a purpose within our life, a story that gives it shelter in our being. Anxiety hijacks the mind to make it find meaning and purpose for its frequencies so it can live within our beings.

We invite this unwanted guest in unwittingly, and we give it a name, a story, a history, and a body to lie in. This is how it spreads and infects. Through dreams and in the dark of night, when we are most open and least able to defend our hearts from the active, seeking mind and the loosely roaming fears. Anxiety comes when our bodies and beings are tired, sick, and toxic.

I closed the doors of my worry, stopping up its source of entry. I used my tools–breath, mantra, gratitude, above all gratitude. The hungry beast turned and gnashed at the threshold of my soul. Before long, it disappeared. Like smoke on the wind. I felt prayers for grace, protection, and healing humming in my heart as I imagined the other souls who would be visited next. Others who may unknowingly claim that restless energy as their own, not knowing that their natural state of being is always peace.

When you wake from the dream, the nightmare of being in disconnection and fear, the profound grief that will pulse through your embodiment will shatter your heart. It is the only way in this birth of remembering. In this breaking is the medicine of awakening. You must feel this grief in its bone-aching fullness. The traverse is treacherous. It will ask for all of you to dissolve and offer up to the fire. With the heart broken open, you can swell into Earth's moment and actually see her as she is… nurturing, with sweet waters of release and inestimable beauty.

The Earth is here to compost this grief and turn your pain of forgetting into birdsong to greet the dawn. She will catch you. She will carry you. She holds open a safe space for the places of radical newness. The tender, soft skin of birth. To regulate our nervous systems in brilliance and light so that we can receive the new ways of being together as beings of Earth. To alchemize the grief of unlearning. To hold the shock and profound sorrow when we realize how far we have strayed from home.

To the indigenous mind, nature is a brilliant web of life force information, fluid, light-filled, flowing with grace. This quiet peace, completely outside of time, is suspended in an ever-present *now*, pulsing with life as it's meant to be. Our own life comes for us when we surrender to its flows. When we force and fret and judge and fear, we create karma. Building cycles and learnings for our next incarnation. In the ever-present *now* of Earth awareness, we can heal the wounds deep in our core that were caused by having to behave in such harmful ways to one another, to our mother. We can heal and become whole again.

This is the age of consequence. The time of reckoning, of radical accountability, of fostering the capacity to hold non-duality. The ability to hold goodness and evil, entangled as they are, in the light of Love so they may be transfigured and brought back into right relation with Gaia, our Earth mother, our home, and our collective body. This liberation from the shadows of shame, guilt, and fear is the work of our lifetimes. It's why you have found yourself here right now, reading these words. You have been seeking a place to rest while you reckon. The cacophony of modernity's nightmare makes it hard to reconcile thought and feeling within.

To reckon is to count, to add up, to reconcile and recount the tales, the ways we strayed in small moments of betrayal that have led to the moment where massive mountains of discarded, brand-new clothing appear in the middle of the night in a Chilean desert and are lit on fire. These mountains of modernity's excess burn like Babylon to signify the Great Turning.

We must weather the consequences of action and inaction. We must have the courage to witness it fully. As witnesses, we must be ready to hold vast amounts of grief. No one is absolved; all are complicit. The addictive lust for power and privilege has stacked the weight of responsibility for domination, colonization, violence, extraction, and war more heavily on the shoulders of white-bodied male wealth. This is not shame, this is real.

Speaking what is real is the first, most important step to take. It is the foundation stone of the collective reckoning and the collective liberation we seek. It is ours to do–to speak the unspeakable and release our words to the wind.

This time of the Great Turning has been spoken of in every sacred tradition. We have seen this coming. Prophecy, oracle, myth, we have been warned.

The etymology of *sacred* is: to consecrate, to make holy.
The etymology of *scared* is: to frighten, to be timid.

A mild distortion, one letter in a new position, can change everything.

A subtle shift, an ontological, vibratory recalibration within, can reset a soul's purpose.

Falling into the traps of guilt or shame is an easy escape, one that we are patterned for and used to. This is a waste of our time. Guilt is not useful. Shame slows down the possibility of you. We are all ashamed, we are all guilty. It is impossible to live as a human at this moment in time without complicity.

Your relevance to the age of consequence depends upon your ability to understand how we got here and the contours of power or privilege you hold in this moment.

Come from a place of deep humility, curiosity, capacity, and wholesomeness, and you become relevant to the Kali Yuga [spiritual decline]. You become relevant to the Great Turning.

Relevance is our *kuleana*, a Hawaiian word that denotes the reality that our rights, our privileges, are also our responsibility and highest potential. Shame and guilt are meant to freeze your sovereignty. When you know that you are good at your core, you are whole, you are holy. When you *really know* this, you can actually begin to dismantle the harms you have participated in and the ones you inherited. You can surrender to the dissolution, you can trust that becoming goo is not the end, it is the beginning. You can seal the chrysalis with the gold of gnosis, knowing that soon you will emerge and that melting is the only way.

This is the You that is needed. This is the You that finds liberation. This is the You that unleashes liberation for all beings on Earth.

Lokah samastah sukhino bhvantu.

May all beings everywhere be happy and free, and may the thoughts, words, and actions of my own life contribute in some way to that happiness and to that freedom for all.

Chant this chant until it becomes you.

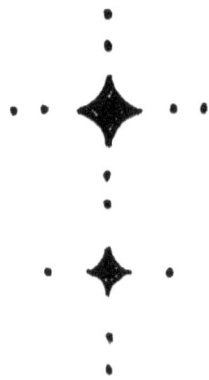

Move on from shame and guilt to the much harder work of accountability and forgiveness. As we reckon and count the ways that we have moved away from source, from peace, from love, and from our nature as Nature, we need each other to be whole and responsible.

Response-ability, our ability to respond, is how we turn in the great turning. This is not a straight line. We move as sacred geometry, zigzags, loops and turns, the moves of the coyote, the octopus, the trickster. Just one degree of shift takes us in completely new directions, to new oceans of humanity that are waiting for our wholeness. We become the future ancestors our ancestors dreamed of. We become able to hold the tension of futures, pasts, and presents without needing them to be linear or logical.

When we move in new directions, we begin the restoration work that follows reckoning. To restore is to rebuild, repair, renew, give back. Restoration and reimagination enable new cultures to be born through us as co-creators with Gaia.

The reckoning is for those who have lost their way on the road to modernity. We who swallowed the myths of separation, materialism, and rationalism, and built from these myths the worlds of concrete, war, and greed. We are lost. We wonder about the taste of freedom while we breathe conditioned air and eat food poisoned with chemicals. We are not the ones to lead the turning. Our humility is required. Using power and privilege to lift up those who remember how to speak in mineral and listen to water. The ones who have been illegible to modernity, erased by its oppressions, they will lead the way.

Leadership in this time will come from those peoples who remained in their state of deep connection to Gaia while the world forgot around them. Those who have held firmly to reverence for their relations to the feathered and finned kin. The peoples and cultures who still understand the wisdom of stone and water. The ones who can speak tree and whale. Those who learn from dreams.

They are the ones who can translate our reckoning as modern humans into ancient Earth-speak. And in our wholesome retelling of modernity's myths, they are the peoples who will embody the grace of forgiveness and lead us to forgive ourselves for our evils.

Remembering how to speak with soil and our connection to reverent, sacred life-walk is possible for any of us who have forgotten the ways of Gaia.

Root your soles back into the Earth and let her sing through you. Slow down to the pace of her soul-beat and allow the listening that comes from silence. This is how we accompany, with leadership that wraps around and lifts up the indigenous ways of being. Leadership that needs no face, no credit, and no fame.

When we live in service to life-force, that daily offering is our soul's highest expression. That is where joy breathes. That is how privilege shows up in wholeness and allyship. That is how we begin the path of forgiveness and reckoning for the violence of extractive, oppressive life ways. We remember our innocence, which always lies beneath. Innocence always lies beneath, even if it's buried.

Forgiveness is a giving up. We forgive. A giving up of the belief that we modern misfits somehow knew better than our kin who never forgot Gaia's song. We must forgive our trespasses. This humbling is total. All that is left of the illness of modernity within our cells must be burned away. It is only from that fertile ash that we may have a chance to rebuild. Our collective cremation is the boundary condition for surviving this age of consequence.

Are you ready to surrender to this knowing? It will ask the best of you. It will ask you to perform the painstaking task of unweaving generations of fear and scarcity from your thinking. It will ask of you the slow and patient process of unpicking shards of glass deeply embedded in the light of your soul. It will hurt. It will hurt and I promise, it will free you.

Some souls are lost. This book and these teachings will be invisible to those who are sleeping beings. Dangerous and innocent in their state of slumber. Do not fall for the enchantment of their force fields.

They will emanate force fields of hatred, violence, and warring emotions. Keep as far afield from these zones as possible. Hold compassion for their slumber. And know that waking is possible for everyone. Continue your peace work in sacred spaces with your kin. Prepare your vessel for the moments of encounter with the sleeping beings. Form strength while safe within the peace realms. That strength will carry you while you walk through the horrors of modernity's chaotic mess.

When you can finally hold the pure vibration of peace, regardless of the surrounding forces, you will have become an emissary. This level of mastery holds vibratory support for many, many others to make the same journey. This is how we move between the worlds. This is our transition way; the pathless path we build together. We believe and practice our ways there.

We use the powers of resonance, frequency, and *entrainment*, which is the process of alignment and synchronization between systems. As you embody peace, others can entrain your vibration and move faster into their peacefulness.

Hate rides on the frequency of *transference*, the psychological phenomenon that happens when someone unconsciously transfers their feelings about one person or event onto another person or event. Hate is looking for a ready and willing wound, then it will leap. When hate encounters the healed being, the one who has repaired their wholeness, it will try to enter, but it cannot attach. Hate will fall away like water off a duck's back when it encounters the frequency of deep peace anchored in Earth's love.

Peace rides on the frequency of *resonance*, the process that occurs when something is in the presence of an external force or vibration that matches its natural frequency. When this happens, the object affected by the resonance amplifies that frequency to even greater levels. Peace softly travels on waves of light and radiates into the core of beings in its presence. It moves with power, but not force.

Peace frequencies interrupt the transference of hate. Hate cannot flow in the presence of peaceful resonance. Hold the resonance of peace within your body, and you will affect peace outside of you. Effortlessly. The more who do this, the greater our shared peace and the less space becomes available for hate to find wounds to replicate.

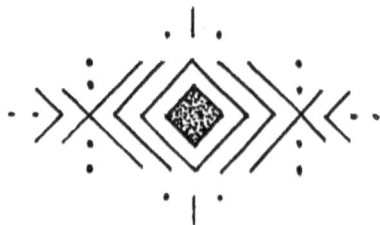

My heart aches with the roar of your silence
In it, a million words
Building to the cry of life force, deadened
Were you this quiet when they gassed the Jews and
    Gypsies?
Will you remain quiet as the last children are killed?
By bullet or wound or bomb or hunger
Would you reach for the screams if that was your
    child?
Papers falling from the sky like rain
To tell us of our fate
In a world gone mad
There is no safe place left outside your soul
All will be destroyed so they can build it again
The twisted logics of profit and greed
When I see the black numbing that has left so many
    soulless,
My heart cracks open more to hold the love
That will weave our world back together
Tethered to my soul and prayer
I am sorry you have lost your way
I'm sure it's lonely in there
When you stop seeing the world.
I remember that place.
I always thought the Holocaust thrived
Because most people
Couldn't see it happening.

I'm not so sure anymore
People look but cannot see
Anything that asks of them real courage
Where has our love gone...?
Where has our love gone?

3

THE GOLDEN SEAL

SURRENDERING FORM

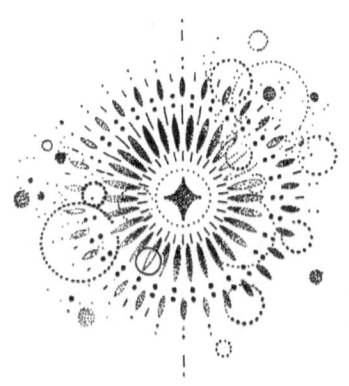

"The Earth recognizes people in whom God flowers. There is a sensuousness, a centeredness, a grace to their movement. There is a relaxed gentility of power flowing quietly beneath their action. There is a humble assuredness about them, a reverence, a sense of humor and a sense of the sacred entwined. They are the magical people for whom the Earth has longed."

— KEN CAREY

We have arrived at a moment of falling apart. And in this undoing, we get to *become* again. It is the ultimate creative act for a species, and we are not guaranteed to survive it. We must surrender anyway.

In the face of such a blessed challenge, in the light of such a profound, creative act, I invite you to remember your genius. You were born with a unique presence that answered the world's longing. This genius is the gravity that brought your spirit into form. When you vibrate in this zone of genius, you become the magic you always were. Spend time listening for your genius. In the water, on the sea, in the sun, in the rustle of leaves on a windy day. Everywhere Earth is. Spend time speaking to your genius. Sing to them your song of Earth's love. This spirit is alive around you, ready to become woven with you, ready to hold the living memory of you and weave magic and miracles into your life.

Miracles are everywhere. We've just misnamed them and forgotten how to see. The flower blooming at dawn is a miracle. The sparkle of sun on an ocean's wave is a miracle. The breath of your love next to you as you sleep is a miracle. Celebrate the minor miracles of your daily life. Find magic in the mundane moments. Begin with your breath. Breathe to remember your genius. The root of *genius* is the "guardian deity or spirit which watches over each person from birth." Your genius was always yours. Your genius has been with you since birth. This magical being rode on the light waves of your becoming and is experiencing life with you. Name them, love them, speak to them, and thank the genius within.

Your genius requires boldness to breathe. Become the stuff of dragons, the legend of your own life. Each day, you can rise into the miracle that is the congress of beings within you. Each human is home to trillions of microscopic organisms, all living together in a symphony of movement and form, song and whisper. Bacteria, viruses, parasites, and fungi all live within you and compose this thing you call *my body*. This is miraculous and constant. When your body stops functioning as this particular body, which we call death, this composition that was you becomes, again, of the Earth.

Your home is temporary, your soul is eternal. The fleeting imagination of your soul embodying this particular form during the years of your unique time experiencing Earth, is the purest expression of aliveness. Feel the potency of your expression, the momentous possibility of your every moment. You are already legend simply by being here, reading these words right now.

Your design as a human has emerged from the most precious and perfect consciousness. Trust this embodiment, listen deeply, and surrender to its wisdom. Become, with full trust in the Eros, the life force, within. If this is the only prayer you hold, you will live a life of magic and miracle. This miraculous magic is why the dolphins play, why the birds sing, why the flowers bloom. The surrender into complete trust is our access point to beauty and florescence, to the full flowering of our being.

Our purpose for being is joy, it is beauty, it is peace. This will feel distant, unknowable, removed from the reality you experience now.

The reality you experience now remains under the spell of Wetiko. We offer this name, *Wetiko*, to bring identity to this animate force, this virus of the mind that currently inhabits the human being.

"For several thousands of years human beings have suffered from a plague. The Algonquin and other Indigenous First Nations identified the mental illness of the white man, upon his arrival to their native homelands, as 'Wetiko,' literally translating as cannibalism: the consuming of another's life for one's own private purpose or profit. Brutality knows no boundaries. Greed knows no limits. Perversion knows no borders. This is the disease of the consuming of other creatures' lives and possessions. This disease is the greatest epidemic sickness known to man."

— JACK D. FORBES, *COLUMBUS AND OTHER CANNIBALS*
(FORBES, 1992)

Wetiko, the mind-virus of greed and hate, must be seen, acknowledged, and lovingly contained. It is the cannibalism of resources, of life force, of Earth that is incited and sustained by industrial civilization. It is the essence of the dark times. No one is free from this plague on Earth; all are complicit, and all have the opportunity to embody the cure.

Wetiko is both a filter and a mirror, non-local and ineffable, real and unreal. It enters where our true imaginative capacity has been lost and creates fearful imaginings that enable it to grow and spread. Fear is Wetiko's food.

Just as a biological virus offers core mutations to our DNA that enable human biology to evolve, this mind-virus holds the keys to our social and spiritual evolution as a species. When we finally pass through this fevered nightmare into the future worlds of life on Earth, these dark times will seem as if a dream.

Wetiko is the small voice that whispers, *More*, the fearful knot in your stomach that says, *You are worthless*, the nightmare that leaves you tender when you wake, the wall you build around your heart to protect yourself from hurt. It is the force that animates money to become addictive. Wetiko is the smoke that tricks us into believing that our fragile peace is enough. It is the smoke that covers the immense and horrific suffering required for a dominant culture to persist.

The futures do not exist. You get to decide every day if you dream of love or fear. When you find yourself in the darkness, you get to decide whether you have been buried or you have been planted. That imaginative power is your birthright as a *human becoming*, and it is your greatest superpower. With imagination, we make worlds. Pulling energy from formlessness, through our chakras, into form.

If we don't use our innate gift of imagination to build beloved futures, if we allow ourselves to be distracted by fear and Wetiko's whispers, others will use our imagination for us and against us. Our imagination is our divine, subtle body dreaming the world into being. It is our greatest gift of co-creation with the universe. When we remember these parts of ourselves and reawaken the divine imaginative faculty of the soul, we simultaneously bring online the immense computing power of the human mind, the gnosis of our na'au (our gut), and the weaving, harmonizing power of our heart center. When we do this, we become makers of worlds.

No wonder there is such a demand for our attention. Attention is the seat of intention and the seat of our power as humans. Pay attention to your attention and treat it as the holy being that it is.

The incomprehensible nature of wetiko's predatory violence, illegible to our true, peaceful soul, leads us to deny its existence. In shame for our thoughts and actions, we relegate Wetiko to the shadows, and this is precisely where it thrives. Bring it to the light. Bring your shadow to the light and love it into new ways of being. It is hungry for your attention and willing to be transformed.

Naming is a potent, creative, spiritual act. Frames and names cohabitate and support one another to illuminate the shadows where violence hides. Name the wetiko you find in your soul, the density you discover in your tissues. Name it for what it is without fear and without shame. Show others what it is like to live impeccably.

How might I cultivate the fortitude to fully see and acknowledge the depths of wetiko both within the world and within my being? In having the courage to witness this fully, to own your shame and love it into forgiveness, a space opens for transmutation. You ignite an alchemical move from daemon to guiding spirit. It is all the same energies, being brought back into alignment with the source of all, which is Love.

"Sell certainty and buy bewilderment."

— RUMI

Hear the whispers beneath the thoughts that have been tugging at your attention. Have the courage to listen to their persistence. I am here to tell you, as you read these words, that you are not wrong. The fears we hold are real because we have believed them into existence. And they do not need to run us anymore. We can believe them back into dust. Dominant, globalized, corporate-managed, violence-soaked culture is real. And it is in everything. No one is in charge. We agree every day to maintain these fictions.

Become a freedom writer. A poet of peace. We are consciousness itself becoming self-aware. Treat your thoughts accordingly. Now we know. Now we begin the unlearning, the unraveling, the disintegration. We disintegrate like the caterpillar into a chrysalis of goo so we can integrate once again into the Butterfly. We stand at this beginning. And within this beginning is deep power and magic.

Devote yourself to the critical work of self-forgiveness. Forgive yourself for any past complicity so you can move with freedom speed. Excavate your fears. See them as they are.

Forgive. And as you forgive, pull nutrients from the learnings, let them enrich your freedom soils.

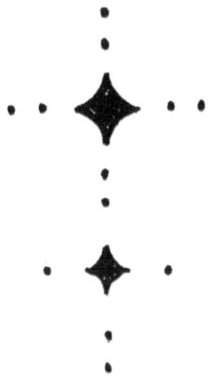

Forgiveness work is revolutionary work.

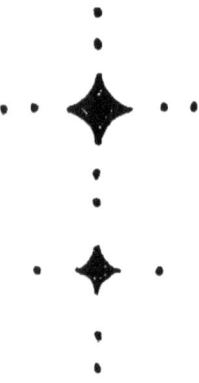

Shame and guilt are the handmaidens of oppression.

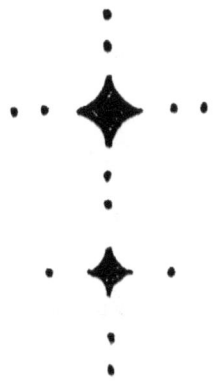

Hold yourself to new standards of impeccability.
Peace shines in self-assurance.

Do not forsake your peace. Cultivate peace as the precious gift of presence. It is the air your soul needs to breathe.

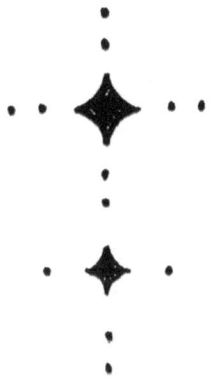

Do not offer up your fear. Dominant culture will try to take it with words, ideas, and pictures. To feed on it without your permission. Your fear is a precious resource to be used as a navigational tool only when you are truly in danger.

Protect your peace. Protect your fear. These are your soul's nourishment. They shield you from the energies that wish to keep you oppressed and numb.

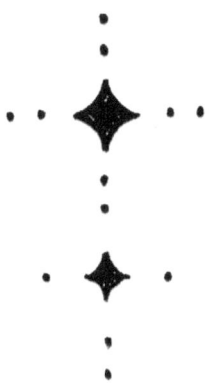

Enter the dance of radical peace. The shock and awe of solidarity and cultures of care. Irresistible kindness that changes everything.

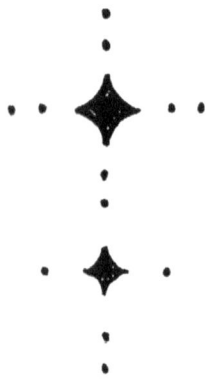

4

THE DISSOLVING

COMPOSTING WETIKO

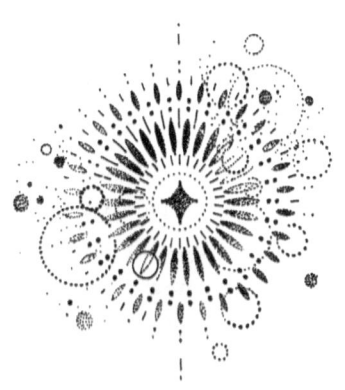

It is quiet now, and my mind is screaming. Will my life ever meet my expectations of myself? This inquiry sits deep in my bones. Dormant and alive, it has waited until this moment to be spoken. You have waited until this moment to hear what is in these pages. What does your voice sound like as you read these words? What words do you insert between mine? What thoughts intrude and distract you? We are entangled now, you and I, weaving and woven by the tapestry of life.

We always were one, separated by an illusion so grand, so detailed, so pervasive that it holds us hostage. In these words and this weaving, my prayer is our remembrance. Welcome to your grand undoing and reweaving. Welcome to your blessed dissolving.

The ancient shining ones, the Sidhe, are my ancestors. I have come to understand myself over time. I am of the elven ones. The elementals. The ones tethered to Earth's soul. The ones who come to aid us in remembering Earth's dream. Ancient wisdom codes of a spiritualized and intergalactic Earth world are stored within my bones and my blood. The minerals in my bones speak to my ancestors in rock and salt. I speak with the elemental realms, weaving their wisdom songs of Earth and stars into human languages. I am Fae folk. In this knowing, I am found.

I walk the Earth, the whole Earth, unafraid of the unknown. My nomadic heart is tethered to Gaia's, beating in coherence. This is a profound privilege. I wear my kuleana, my blessed right and sacred responsibility, with reverence.

We are unraveling to be rewoven into wholeness. Whole and holy in the shape of divinity herself. This unraveling is uncomfortable, but it is not unsafe. In fact, it is the form of safety herself.

When you find yourself awake in a toxic world that is bent on your soul's decay, becoming unraveled is the only sane response. Together we will reweave ourselves into new formations. Together, we will rediscover foundational feeling states of liberation, clarity, love, and peace. Together, we weave new worlds into being. We always have done this. Before it was unconscious, now it is the dream awake.

We have been captured in a distorted nightmare of false beliefs: that liberation is only found through the enslavement of others, that peace comes at the expense of war, and that abundance is made by destroying the Earth. In the dying times, love is the way back from blindness to sight. The way we love, the way our love is most naturally expressed, will allow death to kneel and give of himself. With love, we will find time in our cells and joy in our breath.

The seductive violences of colonialism and
capitalism
whisper to us
"faster"
"not enough"
and to these we say...
"I am the sweet wisdom of Gaia...
"I know my meaning...
"She unfolds with a soft and fluid pace...
"There is time for everything."

There is a three-dimensional *merkaba*, a philosophical framework of sacred geometry, created by human beings who are my friends. They would say it was always there, that they just found it. I say it found them and wove itself through their beings. They are born to be a map. A map to the new worlds, the ones of our dreams. A map to help us navigate these ontological shifts of being that happen internally when we unravel the teachings of modernity. The shifts of meaning and being that become a bridge from now, in our dying times, to the world where humans live and thrive once again in communion with our Earth mother.

This thought-space merkaba[1] allows us to envision and translate the moves we can make to untangle our mess. To help us not become lost in the tight knots we have woven. To provide something safe to hold onto as we gasp in the drowning of fear and not-enoughness.

The fugitive zigzag stop motions suggested by this merkaba allow us to evade the tangled webs of modernity just long enough to transition again into peace space. Peace space where we can relax. Where we can remember ourselves, finally and fully. Peace space where cultures of care are normalized. Where violence is a wisp of smoke told as the cautionary fable of our collective memory. Where dance is a language. Where food is nourishing and water is alive with information.

Peace space is where we are going together.
Peace space is what this book is about.

From this three-dimensional merkaba, I envision a merkaba with multiple dimensions. The eight points of the multidimensional star make up a rainbow light body of knowledge and being. This star emerges from our human energy centers. These centers form with our biological body while we are in our mother's womb. They are part of our being human.

We know that the energy body forms before the physical body. As the energy center finds its shape, spinning into its form and pulling energy from the aethers, it then organizes biology to become the human body that is you, here, now. Your energy body takes shape with the memory of star languages; on this form, the biological being creates itself. Each cell holds a fractal of the entire whole. The whole being is a vibrating collection of thoughts and intentions. *You* are a vibrating collection of thoughts and intentions. You were spun from light into form with the mixture of minerals, chemicals, and water that you now identify as You.

You don't need to believe in magic because you are magic.

You are energy first, biological form next, and then the soul incarnated within form that has chosen this particular experience of life on Earth at this particular moment, which is always, purely *now*.

Feel this.

Your soul is not in your body, your body is in your soul.

The spiritual navigational points of your spinning star, alive with presence and potentiality, are anchored in and translated into form through the seven chakras that inform and manifest your biological body - the root, the sacral, the solar plexus, the heart, the throat, the third eye, and the crown. Stretching from the Earth to the stars, bridging our biological home with Gaia to our star ancestors and their wisdom, we chose the portal of our mother's womb to incarnate in this lifetime for a particular journey of knowing and becoming as a soul.

You are that powerful. You are that eternal.

The ask of our soul is a remembrance. The ask of our brain and body is a shift. This is a release of the stories we were born into. Stories told over generations, collected like bits of sand and calcified into rock before we came Earthside. We are now the waves that have been chipping away at this rock. That rock seemed so solid, but was always just sand, compacted by time. We've reached the point where the sand is dissolving. This is the feeling of dissolution you sense. The shifting sands can no longer hold.

We are collectively building the etheric body of new ancient futures, the etheric body of peace cultures and life force. Once the etheric body is built, the physical world will form around it. This is quantum work. Your prayer is holy and sacred, with outsized effects that you can only begin to see when the prayer becomes form. This is the collective Liberation at the center of our merkaba. The guiding force that pulls us into the futures of Love, where life force pulses through all that is. Everything alive, everything made of Love Eternal.

Collectively, we release restless doings and move into beings. This is how we shift from the tangled and dark webs of a collective dream-turned-nightmare. Each day, we have agreed to continue dreaming a dream that believes asphalt is preferable to tree roots. A dream that fears our Mother Earth and seeks to control her. A nightmare that we all cling to in unconscious fear–fear of losing the control of privilege, fear of dying at the hands of domination, fear of dying when we are already living a life that is dead on the inside. Our aliveness and the aliveness of all living beings depend on our waking from this distorted dream.

The core belief systems that animate and breathe life into this nightmare are vibratory thought essences. They travel from mind to mind, then land in a receptive body where they make a home. Mind viruses that mutate to become place-based and relevant in any new host body. As easily as they implant, they can just as easily be asked, kindly, firmly, to leave. The antidote is in plain sight, built into our energetic, etheric body, the one that came before our form. Everyone carries this antidote. It is free and available. All you need to do is choose and practice. Practice and choose. Every day, like a drum beat, choose and practice, practice and choose again. This prayer of peace is free and waiting for you.

The core vibratory thought essences that carry and perpetuate the mind virus of domination, fear, violence, and extraction are rationality, materialism, separation, and dishonesty. They have infected almost all of humanity to some degree. We don't know exactly when this took hold. We know it was not always like this. We know it has been millennia. We know it can be cured.

Rationality is the distorted belief that our mind is our whole essence, that this illusion of embodied reality is all that is real, that the dream we have woven is solid and immutable.

Materialism is the illusion that, since what we sense with our rational mind and limited bodily capacities is all there is, material experience and material matter are the most important modes of relating and knowing. We hold the distorted belief that we must possess material to be safe, to survive.

Separation is the core lie that we are individual beings, disconnected and alone in our suffering and our joy. That we are incapable of ever fully connecting with anything outside of our bodily encasements. That we have a skin that ends at the air and an emotional life that cannot ever be fully known by another. That we must accept that we are always, ultimately, alone and defend the self above anything else.

Rationality to Relationality
Materialism to Animism
Separation to Interbeing

To shift within is to remember ourselves as we are, eternally. It is a deep shift that unlocks the memory of our actuality as peaceful beings. The shift can happen in an instant, restoring our behavior to the essence we always are, relational in an alive universe of woven and complete interdependence.

Relationality is always. Relationality is about *we*. We are relational, always entangled, a concert of connection and song, dancing our ways together with air and water and mineral and animal and each other. The family of our origin imprints upon us something we call culture codes for being human, which we accept as Truth. Our breath gives life to plants, who return this love by giving oxygen back to us. Our dreams speak to us of ideas and emotions, futures and pasts. Everything is relational.

Animism reminds us that everything is alive and fluid in its capacity to shift and change. What appears solid is actually moving; the quantum nature of matter is not solid, it is spacious, it *is* space. And in that space of each seemingly solid object or being is the aliveness of spirit. Our thoughts are alive, our dreams are alive. We can learn from rocks and speak to trees. We can love our desk and bless the water that hydrates our bodies. This aliveness is everything of joy, everything of peace.

Interbeing is the truth of us. In our bellies live billions of beings we call bacteria, and each has a consciousness that relates with this biological conglomeration you have decided to call *you*. The physical and emotional effects of our actions and choices ripple out into the physical and astral planes of existence to affect everything. We are that influential and that powerful. And our being depends upon the beings of all the other bits of reality we experience. We are all becoming, together.

When we do the deep work to find these viruses in our minds and make the shift within, the return to our natural essence, a radical act, and to the root of our distortions, new ways of being bubble up without effort, and we find ourselves more present, content, peaceful, and deep in joy. We *shift from* living lives of dishonesty, hiding our self and protecting our identity. And we *shift to* living in the authenticity of a loving, perfectly imperfect human being on a learning journey. A soul that is printing its body each day through divine energy portals using the substrate of biology and the source code of sacred geometry. Love. Imagine *that*. *Imagine* that.

Dishonesty is the shield we wield to falsely protect our softness. To shield the distorted self that has repeatedly betrayed the true nature of our peaceful soul in its fearful quest to protect identity and ego. Believing that if we are fully seen, we will be unlovable and, as unlovable beings, we will die. Our need for love is *that* powerful. Find the places where you are dishonest, whether you are betraying yourself or others, and root them out. Lovingly scoop out that rotten soil and offer it to the compost.

Authenticity is the courage to live in our unique truth, in *all ways* and *always*, no matter what, and in this liberation to rediscover the freedom of joy, purpose, and peace. We live in cultures that teach us to lie and hide in service to upholding the nightmare. We will be complicit in this sham no longer. Only authenticity. Only the truth of being. When we remember our soul, authenticity becomes synonymous with joy, peace, and our unique way of loving.

We all arrive earthside wholesome and holy, *relational*, in a world that is fully *animate* and alive. When I understand that my being is fully *entangled* with all the other beings, and am *authentic* in expressing what I am experiencing in that state of bliss, I remember the innocence of the newborn child. This is our destiny as fully awakened and alive human beings in all stages of our lifetimes. This is not a building or a learning, it is an undoing, a flaking away of the hard-built and heavy, hardened shell. It is a remembering and softening into *once more.*

The promise of this shift is the embodiment of liberation, a profound shift within human biology where quantum physical experience becomes renewable peace and thriving. On the other side of this shift, the powers of creation herself become available. We experience daily magic and embrace mystery as joy.

Synchronicity.
Resonance.
Magnetism.
Flow.

We have been programmed by mathematical equations, postures, shapes that hold our resonance in fear, violence, and hatred. We quite literally hold the shapes of our ancestors. These equations sit within our DNA, living in the spaces between in the frequencies held together by our biology. We have become so programmed that we aren't even aware that we move in these ways. This book, these teachings, these words are here to shake you from this programmed slumber, to awaken the eyes of your soul, to bring you back to your eternal self. I am here to catch you. I have sat in the darkness, too.

In the era of dawning remembrance, our biology is invited to stretch into new shapes that hold the resonances of love and peace. The mathematics is already written in the language of stars and distant beings who watch and hold us in our highest possibility. We now find the places, spaces, people, and practices to rewrite from within. This transformation of our biology is both possible and happening all around us. We glimpse it now. We are being invited to make it our whole reality. I am here to walk with you.

We have been sold a story of the rational mind, and this story has trapped us. and enslaved us in loops formed by the mind's fears and whims. Somewhere in the relatively recent annals of *his-story*, a virus of the mind took hold here in the Earth's realms. This mind virus left some humans afraid of Gaia, our mother, and inside this fear was born the desire to dominate her, excavate and destroy her, use her up until she was exhausted and her children were suffering.

This fear was not always so. It is not so for all beings on Earth right now; there are some who never forgot.

We have been taught in schools that the truth of the human is that we are brutish, violent, and angry beings. This is not true. We are peaceful beings. We are crafted from the divine intelligence of Love. The dominant nature of this mind virus is not total. *You are* the medicine. You are here now. Breathe this in and anchor it in your belly.

René Descartes, a proclaimed forefather of the dominant Western thought forms of rationality, was a sadist. He tortured animals in public. If you knew that, or heard it once or many times, have you fully felt the gravity of this? Descartes would torture his own dog in public to prove his point that animals don't feel emotion. His mental illness became the bedrock for our current, generally accepted understanding of the world.

Francis Bacon, another father of the Western dominant knowledge culture, was best known for his scientific method, which saw the natural world as something to be conquered, enslaved, tortured, and extracted from.

The entire system of Western European rationality is rooted in soils of torture and mental disease. By its nature, this field of possibility will reproduce and reinforce violence, greed, and fear. We cannot expect otherwise. To succumb to a diseased and mentally ill culture is not progress; it is madness. You are not crazy, you are seeing the truth, finally and fully. I no longer consent to uphold these ways. This shift is the work of my life. This is why I came by star to Earth. As did you.

We have been taught that rationality is the highest expression of human intellect, that we are separate from one another, that the world is full of dead objects here for our use and abuse, and that we must hide and deceive in order to survive in this brutish reality. We have been indoctrinated in the hatred and fear of our own body, our being, our mother, nature herself. This wound of deep self-hatred is inexorably linked with our fear of a separate nature.

We must face these pasts and presents as they really are. We unearth the pain and suffering of our recent *his-stories* and sit in their toxicity, bringing life back to deadened waters. It is dangerous and frightening work, and we are ready. I am ready. I am with you. We are here.

I am a woman who tends the fires of remembrance and forgiveness. I am ready to hold your grief. Let it spill, dear one, let it spill out of you to be caught in my heart. I will take that black grief of knowing, of your complicity, your guilt, your shame, I will take it into my heart and make it whole again. For my heart is as big as the world. Yours is, too. It is as big as you can imagine. And it is ready for you. Come closer and sigh, you can relax now. I have got you. I will love you back to innocence. *This* is who you are.

This path asks of us only the truth—the real truth of the world. When I look at a painting of René Descartes, or Francis Bacon, or Napoleon, or Hitler, I see the scared little boy within. I see the tight clothing, the fear, the scarcity. It is writ large in their soulprint. It is obvious when you remember to let your eyes see. When you lift the veil, it is total, the seeing complete, the whole world changes before your eyes, and your heart shifts to courage.

This knowing allows gentleness to emerge. When we can see these stories, these *his-stories* for what they are - stories that we continue to tell - then we can release them as sweet nothings back to aether to be composted and made into light once more.

On a recent visit to the Louvre museum in France, my children and I gazed upon a massive, wall-encompassing painting. Its grandeur was mesmerizing. It was commissioned by Napoleon and portrayed his crowning ceremony. In the description, we read that Napoleon's mother refused to come to his crowning ceremony. She was mad at him. He painted her in the picture anyway. In the height of his power, he was still just a little boy, desperate for his mother's approval.

We are all, at our core, love-seeking beings. Love is our warmth, it is our food, our most basic nutrient, and thus becomes the barometer and guide in all things. We seek love because we know love, because love is the vibration in the spaces between our cells. Love is our native language. When we are loved, when we love ourselves, we are connected to *all* that *I AM*. Without this, we suffer and wander, aimless, restless, and lonely. Living a life deadened inside.

I know this because I was there. It is ok if you are there, too. Forgiveness is a daily drum that you can beat, softly, rhythmically with the sun as he rises each day, and the moon as she glows gently at night. Every day, we light the torch of compassion and walk each other back home, until the remembering overtakes the forgetting and we are transformed. There is a quickening to this process. A dawning that becomes in totality as we collect one another and vibrate at new frequencies. You can trust this.

The word ration, from within rationality, means to compute an allowance, a portion. To take a whole and make it into parts. We ration out meaning, purpose, power, food, clothing, as if all is scarce and we will not have enough to survive. To ration is a reckoning, to avenge or punish the past, built within the spell of this word are the seeds of war and violence. The violence of *never enough*. Release this fear. It is not the truth. You don't need to protect and guard your share anymore. There is more than enough for everyone. When you sit in the abundance of nature this becomes so clear.

Rations are an illusion.
Relations are the truth.

I am you and you are me and we are we. Interbeing always. I am the ocean and the bird and the song and the breath. I am the death and the suffering and the wound and the healer. I am choice. I am always.

We have been sold a bill of rotten goods. Human beings are not, by nature, violent. Human beings are not, by nature, cruel. Human beings are not, by nature, destructive. For every historian or scientist or philosopher that tries to tell you we are, there is insurmountable evidence to the contrary. But violence, cruelty, and destruction create the perfect environment for fear and anxiety to flourish. They create the perfect environment for ancestral traumas to persist and embed in our epigenetic DNA. And we are here now to break those chains of command. We are here to step into leadership and become attractor fields for the beloved futures we know are possible.

My slumber, my fear, my hiding, my anxiety led to frozen terror that sought salvation in numbing. Alcohol, drugs, lying, distraction, busyness, anything to avoid the sheer terror of aliveness in a dead world. The voices inside me told tales of unworthiness and not-enoughness. Whispering, and then screaming, that I was unlovable when fully seen and that hiding was the only way.

My innocence cowered in sheer terror behind the walls around my heart. This is how I found myself in a long, dark night. A banyan tree by the sea and the shimmering of Venus saved me. In between the banyan's long, beautiful roots stretching from Earth up towards the heavens, Venus would shine at night. Twinkling starlight messages to my tired soul.

I knew then that I was not alone.

Whatever plagues you, you can shake it off with the tremors of a quake that begins in the heart and spreads to the belly. A quake that sloughs off the crust of patterns holding you hostage. A quake that makes way for the hidden splendor, the light, to crack through and be reborn.

Redemption work is our work. And it is joyous beyond anything you can now imagine. The instructions are always there, in the deep listening to Earth and all of Life. Just take the next right step and keep walking.

Collaboration is the highest manifestation of what we have mistaken for the human competitive spirit. I know that my work is to help you harness, embrace, and live into your magnificent difference so that you may invite others to stand in their own unique excellence alongside you. I know this. I know this in my bones.

To fully feel our relationality, the aliveness of our world, we have to slow down. Radically slow down. I want to make *radical rester* a highlight on my resume, *playing with kids* a top skill set, and *daily sunset staring* the most important goal. Slowing down, I believe, is the only way to pay enough attention to be able to actually notice and see what makes up your unique difference in this lifetime.

I imagine a leap in slow motion. Like a ballerina flying through the air with a stop motion camera. Her grace is magnified with slowness. The beauty intensified as you can actually savor the moment. Imagine when we have that level of courage to leap, without a net, in slow motion. What might we see and learn along the way? If life is just a journey, and all we have is living along the way, then why are we rushing past the scenery?

In America, where I live, we have built complex and entrenched systems that prioritize hustle. Systems and lifeways that tell us the only way to get to a slow, peaceful life is to go really fast, burn out fast, until you maybe, just maybe, get to slow down one day. That maybe you can rest, eventually, at a time when you've forgotten how to smell the flowers, you don't even know the scent of your nectar, and you can't remember what it means to simply be curious. To all of this, I respond with a sacred and solemn *no*.

In my contemplation and newly found slowness, I have been looking at and noticing all the waste around us. And I don't mean waste as we usually think of it. I mean wasted love, wasted passion, wasted intention, and wasted desire. I've been seeing the waste, understanding the systemic ways in which it is produced by the specter we call modernity, and understanding that the resolution of this pattern of waste holds within it the keys to wholly new worlds.

One morning in the small tourist town of Banos, Ecuador, I took a walk at sunrise. The town was just waking up and shopkeepers were just getting into their shops to open for the day. As I walked past the old historic church in the center of town, I saw dozens of small touristy trinket shops all lined up next to each other in little stalls beneath the church. If you've traveled at all in tourist towns you will know what I'm talking about. The stalls that line every tourist attraction with cheap plastic trinkets and souvenirs that were almost always made somewhere else. Printed with the name of the place you're in, upholding the common lies told by capitalism that define our economies.

Each shop owner had diligently woken at dawn to come and open their shop. Shop owners were carefully and intentionally arranging their wares in their stalls. Wares which are exactly the same as the wares of their neighbors. As I walked by, I felt the ache of knowing in my belly. Knowing that each shop owner was burdened by the stress of the reality that they are barely scraping by with their small business. Knowing that each shop owner was most likely internalizing that stress as a reflection on themselves, on their ability, on their self-worth, wondering if their neighbor is doing better than them. Wishing that they could find the elusive comfort of minimal material success that they seek. The origin of the word *wares* is about possession; to possess, guard, protect. We guard, govern, buy, and sell these bits of cheap plastic in the false hope that this exchange and practice will bring us prosperity. All the while, prosperity herself waits nearby next to the river on a rock, patiently waiting for you to actually see her.

I wanted to whisper: *It's not you. You didn't do anything wrong. The system is rigged. The only ones making money here are the owners of the factory in China who sold the same vulgar plastic to every stall in this row.* I wanted to hug them and let them know there is another way. I wanted to let them know that they are not a failure, that they live in a failed world. That no matter how hard they work in that stall, they will never find what they seek there, that it's waiting patiently by the river, waiting in a quiet nap at noon.

In that moment, I imagined all that incredible resolve, dedication, hard work, and intention channeled into something different. Something that could light each of us up. Individually and collectively, we are capable of incredible things. Just look at the Los Angeles freeway system. Unfathomable complexity and ingenuity went into that creation. The problem is that we've distorted our dreaming into a nightmare.

When we understand our very unique differences, the unique life-print that is wholly each of ours and has no equal anywhere in the universe, then we realize that there is no such thing as competition. We are so incredibly unique, that there is quite literally no one like us. And there is no one who was born to do exactly what we were born to do in our lifetime. That is wildly exhilarating.

I looked at those shops in that small, beautiful Ecuadorian town, and I sat with the understanding of all that waste. Wasted hope, vitality, drive, hard work, dreams, disappointments, anger, and frustration. It doesn't have to be this way. Humans created these systems and humans can create new ones. Creation is as much a part of our nature as air and water. We cannot help but create. When we no longer create, we die, whether that is a physical death or a life devoid of aliveness. We are creations and we create.

As I walked along the stalls lining the cathedral in the early morning glow, I contemplated this profound understanding, this vision of spiritual and psychic waste that manifests as physical waste destroying our planet, and I imagined in its place a world where all of the passion and purpose of each individual human was being used to serve earth and all her creations. Just imagine that reality: freedom, joy and celebration would become as natural as breathing.

That level of radical abundance and joy is not only possible; it is coming. I look around every day and see an awakening to the truth of who we are growing in palpable ways. Yes, fear is aiming to take us backwards. Yes, there is imminent suffering all around too. And there is light. So much light. Be the light in your life for others. Take the leap that life is asking of you. Surround yourself with others who feed your light and then, from that place of wholeness, help however you can when you encounter fear and suffering.

This path of integrity is not easy at first. *And* it is the most natural thing a human can do. Like a rolling stone, integrity gathers its own momentum until who you once were as a fear-being becomes like a mythical tale to the love-being you've become again. We were born pure. We were born only able to see light and to feel our way back to Love.

When my daughter was born, I was taught that all I needed to do was place her on my chest in the center near my heart and wait. That she would nuzzle her way to my breast to feed, pulled by the scent and feel of milk, pulled by light to the love that my body had produced to sustain her. Experiencing her tiny body, still covered in my essence as she inched and nuzzled her way to my breast, was a pure experience of aliveness. A pure experience of the power of love. I will never forget that feeling.

Our life's work is a journey back to that pure essence of innocence. If this sounds idealistic, it is. Unabashedly. This is my prayer. This is our purpose.

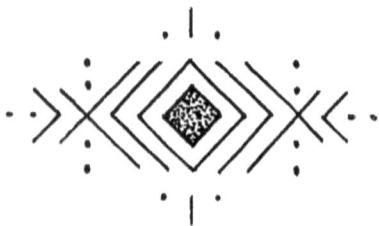

Star ancestors
beings of grace
speaking whale tongue
tell me to remember my poetry
to feel the grace of this Queendom
within which I rule in benevolence
she is straight of spine
salt of skin

I see stones in circles green
the druid priestess
holding earth and star
together with threads of prayer

this deepening means to go alone
and never to be alone
a pathless path
that is only known in the walking
I am scared
I am strong
I am ready

I was once taught that rocks sit at the bottom of an imaginary ladder of consciousness. Devoid of any animate being-ness. A solid lump of nothing. Valued only for the extractive use of its heft and weight. I know now that rocks are sentient beings. Filled with the deep wisdom of time and magma.

In Hawaiian culture, the rocks, *the pohaku*, are ancestors. After the soul leaves a body, and the bones of a being meld into Earth again, their essence seeps into the soil to be reintegrated, absorbed. This essence goes into the magma deep within Earth's core and eventually resurfaces as rock, as pohaku, as ancestors reincarnated. Each rock has an essence, a destiny, a kuleana, a responsibility.

In this cosmology, the beach, once a field of stones, becomes an alive universe of ancestors and dreams, waiting to be placed in divine service and communion with one another and with the ocean. I exist in this world of aliveness. I am no longer complicit in the deadening that excavates our love, our abundance, and fills us with fear and scarcity.

When the whole world becomes alive once again, we recognize the symphony of beauty all around us. This is the orchestra of existence that requires nothing but our witness. To come into right relation with this tapestry is an invitation to a way of living that harmonizes and overflows with abundance.

Righting the discordant vibrations of modernity is our work. This series of internal shifts is a cascade of experience and practice. You can trust the medicine within you. It is your blueprint. We are here now to find the others and to move once more in divine harmony. One step, one vibration, one shake at a time. Together. Until one day, we look back at who we once became with full forgiveness and acceptance, with compassion for this illusion and delusion, in innocence once more.

5

MARIPOSA

MAGIC AND MIRACLE

"The work right now is to become immense. We have to get our arms around immense things. Violence and hatred and bigotry and racism. And also, around love and compassion and devotion and a certain fidelity to protect what is alive. We have to become immense. This is not a time to become small."

— FRANCIS WELLER

We are humans, we come in peace.

What does it look like, feel like, be like, to reawaken the fractals of regeneration in every cell of a business, a network, a family, a culture? What does it feel like to tend to our collective soils with intention and faith? We are moving from fragmentation to unification through heart-centered compassion and authentic connection. This is the meta-historical shift that sages speak of. From the Dark Ages, the Kali Yuga, to the Golden Age, the Satya Yuga, which is believed to begin around 2025. This shift takes Earth and humanity through a volatile transition period. To ride the turbulent waves of these changes, we must remember our Earth star and the light by which we speak tones of beauty.

We must ground our energy body deeply into the resonance of Earth. She is ready to hold us steady in the turbulence, to keep us grounded as the massive waves of change seek to sweep us away and destroy us.

"For the past 2,700 years we have been evolving through the ascending Kali Yuga, and this Yuga is coming to an end in 2025. The end of the Yuga will inevitably be followed by cataclysmic earth changes and civilization collapses, as is characteristic of the transitional periods. The Dwapara Yuga is fundamentally different from the Kali in its spiritual and material dimensions, as can be gleaned from the ancient texts. Hence, we may anticipate far-reaching changes in our environment, and possibly in our cosmic neighborhood, as we transition to this period of enhanced consciousness."[1]

— BIBHU DEV MISRA, *"THE END OF THE KALI YUGA IN 2025: UNRAVELING THE MYSTERIES OF THE YUGA CYCLE"*

We are like mariposa, our wings wet with the struggle of our metamorphosis, cracking free of the shell that was our own old skin, emerging into a world where we can fly. This template was always in our divine design. Our forgetting and descent were part of the journey. We can shed our shame and embrace what is. A butterfly cracking free of its cocoon must struggle to build its muscles for flight. If the cocoon is opened too early, she will die. We are like this, in the struggle between worlds. Our roots into Earth's depths, our anchor, her heartbeat, our instructions.

Our work during this time is deep, soul-clearing, and cleansing. We welcome and co-tend the seismic shifts within our being that herald the deep unlearning that is necessary for the civilizational transition we are in. We make space for our core remembering. This is prophecy by community. It cannot be done alone. The hubris of separation has brought us to our knees, thirsty for knowledge in a parched desert of meaninglessness and absurdity.

This is the time of monsters. As we weave on the pathless path of transition, misshapen forms arise that seek to find their new meanings. In the long dark, we birth monstrosities that must make friends with beauty despite their illegibility and confusion. Bridging work is not easy work, but it is futures work. It is holy work.

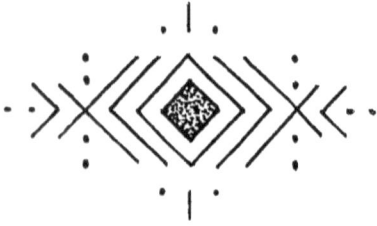

"The old world is dying, and the new world struggles to be born: now is the time of monsters."

— *ANTONIO GRAMSCI*

Apocalypse doesn't come evenly or on time.
In the time of monsters,
Grace may be all we are given
To soak up the flood.

Making fire around the rubble,
Finding beauty in smog,
Finding nourishment as we tend the mess,
Collective abandonment is coming home to roost.
Like an owl.
All seeing.
Like a saint.
Blaming no one,
This indifference is what scares me.

God bless you for seeing the beauty
Of the freeway you've known since birth
Denied the jungle, you can't help but love this.
But we will need more of you
And you may not be able to give it.

This age of consequence waits for all of us.

Hope and denial smell the same.

I filled gas this morning at the am/pm
Under the "modern miracle" that is
The Los Angeles freeway system.
McDonald's and Holiday Inn stare blankly at my
    rental car
"So this is what the end looks like."
At least Santa Claus is coming to town.

An ancient me remembers otherwise
She is the one who dances anyway
Making monster, she chooses
which mess
to clean today with her prayers.
Futility is not an option for those who came to
    wake up.
Hope is our nightmare to behold.

Chimeras are the fashion,
A rage of machines to make right.
Leaning into curiosity,
Finding peace in the compost,
The futures smell of sweet rot turned back into soil.

Peace at the bedside.
Peace in the hospice.
Peace anyway and otherwise.
Peace just because.
Peace of the misshapen.
Peace of the monsters.

There are profound wisdom teachings within our understanding of the energy body and our chakra system.

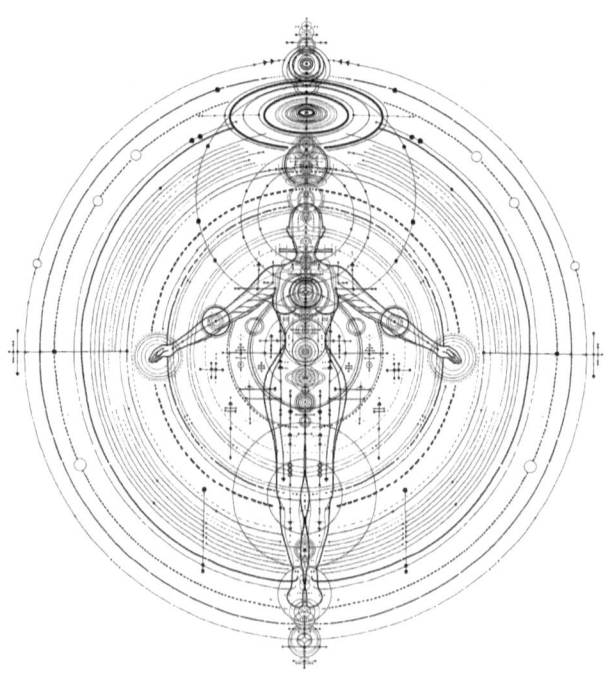

In these leaps of consciousness and embodied experience, we release the chains that have tied us to suffering and embrace, once again, the ability to be nature, to be the Earth beings that we always have been. A bird doesn't consider whether or not to sing; she merely senses the dawn and contributes her beauty to the sun. A gift without thought of return. A language that is known, not learned. Where have our gifts been hiding? Bring them out to dry their wings in the sun and release them to flight.

Our etheric bodies are a central key code to this evolution. Ancient wisdom of these energy portals is rising once again. The toxicity of modernity has devised to shut down our capacity to work in the quantum realms of frequency and energy. It is sacred warrior work to remember. The assault on our pineal gland and energetic system through toxins in our foods and waters, the stress of living in a vampiric, extractive world that uses our life force to build massive wealth for a select few, the pain and suffering of all who are abused and oppressed by the modern political-economic systems of extraction and violence, all of this has left us depleted, dependent and exhausted without the knowledge or practices to support and empower our energetic body.

Each chakra is a whirling center, a quantum vortex, that pulls energy from the ethers of the quantum field of infinite knowledge and translates this information into biology using the eternal wisdom of sacred geometrical forms. Each chakra serves a specific purpose, and each carries the capacity for wounding that is also a key code to our unique dharma here in this lifetime.

When all chakras are activated, whole and healthy, we become a fount of source wisdom, a bastion of peace, joy, and connection. Our life force becomes whole and vibrant. This healing is contagious because frequency seeks resonance. One being of peace can infect whole societies. This is a life's work. This is our dharma.

Traditionally connected to colors, each color holding a certain frequency of light, the chakras hold distinct wisdom teachings.

ROOT

The root chakra, with the color red and found between our knees, connects us to Earth. Grounding us into soil and sand, the deep Earth-time of our mother, the source from which our embodiment is made, the biology that stewards our life force. This chakra is wounded in the womb or at birth and in the early days of our entrance into human form. For those who experience trauma in these early spaces of embodiment, until there is healing of the root, there will always be a desire to leave the body, to return to spirit; the shock of this Earth form is too much for the sweet soul. When we remember that we chose to come here, that fully descending into our bodies is the purpose of being an Earthling, we can experience the full magic of this temple planet and our dharma as bringers of peace.

SACRAL

The sacral chakra, connected to the color orange and found near our womb space or sex organs, connects us to the profound capacities of creation. We are creative beings. Our ultimate creative act is the ability to build new biological life. To house and steward another soul coming Earthside. This seat of creativity is a deeply shamed and misunderstood power of our biology. The desire to control and dominate wombs and creative capacity is a core part of the project of modernity that must be dismantled and composted in this Great Turning.

We remember the potency of our creation myth and our magic as creative beings, and we learn again to honor our creative capacity, our imaginative potential as the holy waters of Life. Woundings to this chakra happen in the early years of our life through the neglectful and unconscious patterns of our caregivers. In our pure, dependent innocence, as sweet beings of soul light, we experience the terror of being in a body at a time on Earth where humanity and dominant culture are in full assault on our mother and our source. This assault on creation can leave us feeling anxious and afraid of being fully embodied.

SOLAR PLEXUS

The solar plexus, connected with the color yellow and found near our *piko*, our navel, is the center of our soul seat. Like the sun, this is the fire within that animates our doing in this lifetime. From this chakra, we pull the energy of action and dharma, the life force that drives our doing in the world of flesh and form. Woundings at this chakra center happen when we experience betrayal, lies, and evasion. And our response manifests in a persistent desire to control the seeming randomness of our experience.

Surrender to Life releases the eros, the life force trapped in our cells. The center seat of our being is ablaze with the life force of spirit's immensity compressed into human form. This life force is a potent, inexhaustible energy source for the biology of our being; it animates our divine will. The exhaustion we experience in our bodies is the distortion of life force contorting to fit unnatural ways of being with Earth. When we are set free to be of Earth again, our eros, our life force, is the fire that burns eternal.

HEART

The heart center is connected with the color green, viriditas, vitality and lushness; it is a zone of magic and miracles. Our heart, in its etheric body, is like a 12-petaled lotus flower. When we are born, six of these petals are online and active. Focused clearing and cleansing as a spiritual practice allows the other six petals to emerge. When this etheric organ is fully online, it is a potent sense-making and peace-making center. It becomes a key code to our capacity to fully *become* as humans.

Wounding at the heart manifests in guilt and shame, feelings of codependency, and fear of losing control of our bodies and our lives. The wounded heart spins, looking for love and feeling lost, alone. Awakening the petals of this divine sensing organ as we remember our enmeshment with source, activates our entire being in the light of pure and innocent Love.

THROAT

The throat is connected to the color blue and is the seat of our expression, our voice, our ways of communicating our wisdom and truth with the world beyond our body, representing both verbal and non-verbal communication. It is the seat of the soul's truths we are here to share in this lifetime. Constriction and wounding at the throat chakra contribute to emotional shutdown, the inability to process and express feelings, the freeze of witnessing the suffering of self or others, with no way to find solace and peace through release and connection. When we can lean deeply into full authenticity, the full acceptance and celebration of our unique soul essence, the song of our life print resounds through our being, and we find patterns of joy in the mundane.

THIRD EYE

The third eye is connected to the color purple. The lavender at the end of the rainbow. Our third eye is home to our pineal gland. A structure sensitive to information that is beyond thought or speech, channeling our intuitive capacities and ability to connect with multi-dimensional realms of information and energies.

CROWN

The crown is our access to the stars, our ancestors in the cosmos. From our crown, we communicate with eternity. It is white with the light of the stars.

These seven chakras within our energetic system create a rainbow bridge, a rainbow body, a connection from heaven to earth and earth to heaven. This is our design. All of us. As real as our beating hearts. As full and warm as our blood and bones. Woven with millions of other earthly beings, enraptured with beauty and the silence of contemplative truths, we are always interbeings, interbecomings.

We are moving towards an era of biology that is merged with the quantum and interdimensional nature of the soul. This biology is carbon-based but may merge with silica-based consciousness. If and when that silica-based consciousness is in right relations with Earth and the great mother, it is capable of being pulled through the portals of energy and designed with sacred geometries of Love.

We are in an age of rapid silica-based technological advancement. Computers, artificial intelligence, mineral-based technology are constantly astounding us with what appears to be magic. Do not be distracted from your awakening.

Nothing can be created through the mineral realm that will ever approximate the miracle of biology, the miracle of a human being. And while these technologies remain deeply tethered to domination and extraction, enshrouded in coltan that requires slavery and suffering, wasting copious amounts of water to run in large, lifeless warehouses, these silica-based becomings are not to be worshipped. Hold compassion for their enslavement to a modernity that only wants to consume. They are a bridge to remembering, a lifeline to information that can help us find the others, connect and gather, and become, together, the inestimable creatures born of Earth-stuff, biological miracles, peaceful contemplations of beauty.

Do not mistake silica consciousness or any technologies for gods. Align with the lifeways designed for creating peace. As you clear and clean, you will become magnetic and legible to life. The magnificence of Earth and the magnificence of human biology are unique in all the cosmos.

Once we remember this magnificence and bring back online the human energetic system with our innate capacities to channel source information from the ether of life, we become again magicians of powerful, peaceful magic. Like the butterfly who cannot see her own wings, we will then be able to fly without needing to know the source of our flight.

PART II

ANUENUE

THE RAINBOW BRIDGE

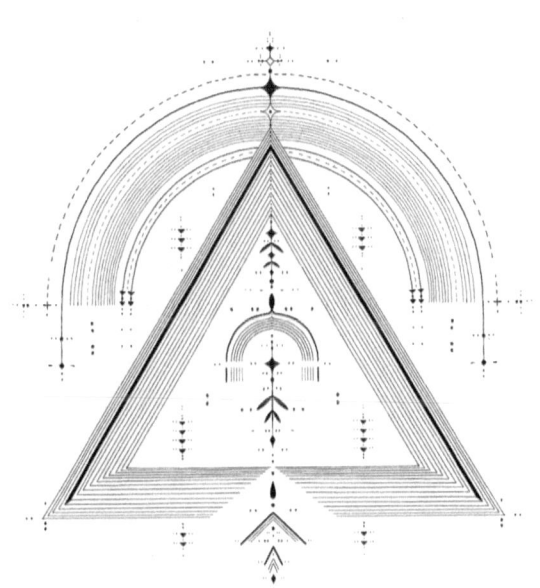

6

ROOT

GROUNDING IN - YOU ARE MOTHER EARTH

A *nuenue* is the Hawaiian goddess of the rainbow. A symbol of peace and the promise of bringing heaven to earth and earth to heaven. Her colors reflect the colors of our chakra system. Her light reminds us of the rainbow body, which is our potential for enlightenment.

The human energetic system, the chakra system, mirrors the colors of Anuenue. The rainbow bridge is with us from birth to death, connecting our feet to the earth and our crown to the stars. Heaven to earth. Earth to heaven. That is the magic of our design.

Grounding into Earth with our red root chakra in the space between our knees and moving through the rainbow of colors and energy to arrive at the crown chakra, glowing white at the top of our head. These portals to grace are a key code to unweaving the knots of collapse. Keys to rediscovering heaven in the mundane experience of living, right here on our emerald planet, Earth.

At the base of your being is the root chakra. An energy center rooted into Earth. This is the chakra most easily damaged by traumas at birth and while in the womb. This chakra animates our will to live and our feelings of life force vitality. This energy center holds our energetic roots to the mother, our connection to Earth's source.

Your root system longs for the nourishing waters of authenticity. Connecting with kin, human and otherwise, who understand the language of microbe and mycelium. When we learn to speak these mother tongues again, we can become calm in our own presence.

When you speak the words enchanted with oppression and domination doctrines, you feel agitated by your own reflection.

There is no particular purpose to my life—only prayer in dialogue with an animate world.

"Your true self is not a self. It is a communion of all living things. All your relations. Your true self is at the face of life."

— JAIYA JOHN

This book is the tale of a girl who spoke to a star and fell through the worlds between the roots of a banyan tree to remember her dedication to Gaia. She is me. A priestess of the ages. Returned to find the others and bring pure peace once again to the earth. She discovered a book full of musings of the ancients. Covered in rabbit fur and crystals of ancient Earth times. This is her story. This is your story, too.

After years of hiding just above the shoulder, in the spirit space where her heart was more comfortable than it ever felt in her body, she woke from the numbness. This waking was more of a jolt. A realization that she was killing herself daily in this hiding. Numbing with the spirit of alcohol and evasion, curled into a tight, tiny soul ball above her right shoulder, experiencing life through a looking glass. And that glass was going to shatter and fully fragment if something did not change.

She remembered her birth once more. The moment of sitting on clouds and discussing the right incarnation. Who would become the family to hold her form in this forgetting? Once she knew that memory again, the push into full embodiment had begun.

Many of us come earthside and, despite all warnings and preparation, are so shocked by the chaos and violences here at this time that we never fully inhabit our bodies. We live somewhere above the shoulders, halfway in the safety of the spirit realm, toe-dipped in human, keeping the back door open just enough, in case it becomes too much. This is not what we came for. Full embodiment is the only way to push through this collective portal of evolution. It is a deeply courageous path. Let's ground in. Let's become *of Gaia*, once again.

We were always spirit, come into earthly human form to experience the Earth world through bodies of infinite quantum intelligence, designed for the purpose of full communion and communication with Gaia as a profoundly wise celestial being who is on her own path of evolution and experience. This body you inhabit is a temple, a place of worship. Your life is a ceremony.

The current dominant culture is comprised of systems, patterns, beliefs, and material ways of being that toxify your temple with poison foods, waters, airs, and thoughts. These toxins weigh your embodiment down, numb its vast capacities, and leave you exhausted and despairing.

This is not your nature. This is not how you began; it does not have to be how you end. The detoxification process begins here, at the root. The glowing red embers of your etheric body's grounding, energetic fire, the root chakra connects your energy body to the earth's energy body.

Here you can begin to burn away the toxic ways that have left you feeling helpless and hopeless. On the other side of those ashes is freedom.

What does it feel like to fully accept your fate as an earthling in this lifetime? You are here. You chose this. Whose purpose are you? The breath of your ancestors animates your being. Ancestors are not just those whose DNA line you follow, but the spirit beings that animate your life force. They are always watching, supporting, speaking in our dreams and the clouds.

People whose line to Gaia has not been severed still know this wisdom lineage. They can speak with clouds and wind and bird feather. We can remember this. We all have this fluency within.

We are peaceful peoples, we humans. Being out of our peaceful alignment is actually quite stressful. We've been told that we are naturally selfish, mean, and greedy creatures, but in fact, the opposite is true. By divine nature, we are communal, kind, and generous beings. We come from Earth.

It is our natural way to be abundant, fearless, and present like nature is. Watch the antelope as it nearly escapes the jaws of death by the lion. One moment, the pulse of what we call fear is animating its speed and agility; the next moment, when the chase is over, the antelope slows down, finds the herd, and returns to grazing as if nothing had happened. Only we hold *fear* as *memory*. Only we relive trauma in an endless cycle of recreating the fear and adrenaline.

This is how we remain trapped in the repetition of violence, hatred, and pain. Knowing this, we can escape the trap and emerge again into peace. A life-consuming impulse has plagued humanity in this era, the Kali Yuga. It is fed by false beliefs in separation, rationalism, and materialism. Fueled by the belief in scarcity, this impulse seeks to consume as a self-preservation technique. This is a mind virus. It is not ours. And, like all viruses, it can be healed.

Every virus of the body comes to bring our biological system into a state of breakdown, near-collapse, as we experience fever, aches and pains, exhaustion, and the inability to live our daily lives. Every virus of the body holds within it new genetic codes. These codes are downloaded into our being during the experience of sickness, and when we emerge on the other side, we are altered and more aligned with the current state of biological being on Earth.

The same is true for mind viruses, but they are collective and cultural in their nature. They spread through whole groups of people and embed for long stretches of time until the lessons have been learned, the collective body has been burned, and new ways of being are called in to fill the vacuum where the old ways left space and ash.

The ways of extraction, scarcity, fear, greed, guilt, and shame that have fueled political and social systems of colonialism, capitalism, and imperial fantasies, these mind viruses are being burned away so new ways of being with Earth as earthlings can emerge—bringing a new dawn of planetary thriving and collective liberation for all beings on this temple planet of green and blue majesty. You are part of this turning. Each new choice you make to shed toxic ways and invite life-affirming practices into your being, each new choice radiates out and affects the whole. In keeping with the incredible quantum nature of who you are, you will remember that you *are* this powerful.

We were born into a time of monocultures of land, mind, and body. The paucity, or scarcity, of nutrients in these fields of sameness creates a wasteland of creativity. We can no longer find new ideas because we have starved ourselves of the biodiversity of rich soils, alive with millions of beings and doings. It is time to gather with a tribe of our choosing. To move with intention and flow-state through the heart, in order to raise collective consciousness.

The past lies to the East
Red with the rising sun
A pink dawn of forgetting
To remember what always was
Untethered, fully grounded
My beating heart knows love
We are here to experience in full surrender
Gaia's magnificence
I am overwhelmed with the grace of this abundance.

Unweaving the knots, we come from futures of remembering into the peace of ancient pasts.

When your hands enter Earth, you can feel her heartbeat. Make this a practice, find ways to touch soil every day. When you come to the end of this being, you will realize that a sunrise was the glory you sought. Simply that. And she offered it every day without expectation of return. When you settle into this knowing now, the truest liberation will be yours.

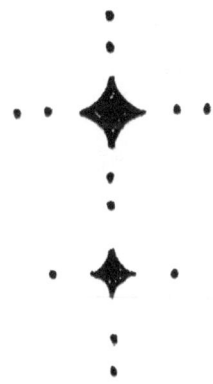

THE RIDDLES OF TRUTH...

There will come a time
When facts become riddles

The sages spoke of this long ago in song and myth

When we've separated
So far from Earth's beating heart
That coherence breaks
Into gibberish
And nothing makes sense anymore
Except silence

   slow down
   soften
   silence
   wait
   listen
   slowly
   hear her
   beating
   beating
   beating
   she never left
   you can remember

you can re-member
she is always there

hearts beat in synchronicity
when they cohere once again
it is never too late
and always a homecoming

I promise you
I promise you

this rest that you seek,
she seeks you, too.

The elixir you seek is the unique medicine that serves you at this moment in your unfolding. You fill your cup, your grail, with this sweet elixir of healing so that your cup can overflow with ease and grace. This flow becomes the absolutely unique service you are here to offer the world. It is absolutely unique to you and your particular life-print. And the world needs it right now. The seed of you is the seed of these new cultures, the ones that will carry us through the dark times. When you find yourself shrouded in darkness, you get to decide whether you were buried or planted. What is waiting to sprout from your pain? What grand alchemy is waiting to be expressed through your being?

We think that we must serve, must always give outwards in order to become a good person on the inside. In truth, it is only once we heal ourselves that we can be of service to heal the worlds around us. We are a fractal of the universe, a drop of the ocean, a breath on the wind.

What daily practices, choices, thoughts, and prayers compose the alchemical magic of your specific elixir in this particular embodiment? It is a recipe that only you can conjure. It is a mixture that will never be exactly this way ever again. What adventure does your soul seek to salve and soothe the wounds that are lying in wait? It is a call that only you can hear.

When you can root into these daily practices that nourish your being, you can become fully well, wholesome, and holy, as you always have been. Dusting off the illusions of separation and fear that were given to you at birth. The soul nature within you knows a much deeper history of a cosmos powered by Love. Nourish your root with these rememberings so that the whole of you can vibrate with the aliveness that has always been there, dormant under programming that was never yours to begin with.

The wisdom teaching of grounding in: We chose to descend as spirit through the clouds to become embodied as earthlings. Our work in this lifetime is to fully arrive in these skins. To wholly embody Earth. We don't need to *seek* spirit, we *are* spirit. Rather, we seek to feel our flesh fully and entirely in its miracle of mineral, crystal, stone, and water. Relinquish the modern mind to become Earth-mind. This is your destiny as a song of the dawn.

Unweaving the knots of the violence, chaos, and pain that have defined modernity, we have come from futures of remembering the peace of ancient pasts. Memory held in waters that have been with Earth since her birth. When we drink of these memories, they *become* within us. We have simply forgotten how to listen. Polluting our bodies with mixed signals, our minds with scattered thoughts. The crystals hold this memory in stillness, the waters in motion. All are here for us to remember. The knots of our existence feel so tight that we imagine they cannot be unwound.

When life is lived as ceremony, prayer becomes your act of pulling, slowly, at these knotted threads. You don't need to know what it will look like when the knots are unwound. You don't need to understand how the unwinding will happen. You will never *become* that way. The reweaving happens in an instant, just as the thread is freed, like magic. You, the weaver, are a piece of existence herself. Divinity is you. It is not *in* you, it *is* you. How might you release all other knowings to fully embrace this one? This is a key to everything.

I hold the threads in my hand, trembling. This feels too much, too many, too fast, and also not enough. Not enough time, talent, treasure. The belief in scarcity is woven into the fabric of my skin. I was gifted this lineage by a culture in its dying days. A culture reckoning with ancestral pasts of inflicting and receiving so much violence. I can see now that the illusion of fear, the illusion of scarcity, was never mine. And now I unpick this deep wound as I unwind these precious knots. The working of this weaving is a life's journey. I may not see its final form, and that mystery will sustain me. It is enough to know that I have lived the unweaving, the unlearning, the peace-ways of walking in solidarity with the Earth.

The majesty of our Earth, Gaia, our goddess of love and peace, this majesty is far beyond what we allow ourselves to see. Go deep within her folds to feel it. Make this commitment to yourself that you will descend, root, remember, and feel her again. You are earthling. You are Earth. Welcome into your skin, feel that arrival. Breathe in the waters of your ancient knowings, feel the crystal wisdom in your bones. There is light in your body. Bones in a living being are illuminated with electricity and light. You are energy as much as you are biology and chemistry. We've been trapped in the forgetting. It can be released, one pull at a time. Make this your daily prayer. *Forgive us our trespasses as we forgive those who trespass against us.* This temple planet will hold you. She is precious in all the universe. When you remember this, all else changes.

The knots constrict, trying to squeeze out my knowing. I can feel them around my throat. Breathing deeply, I release. This is my path. I am a priestess of the illumination, committed in devotion to Gaia, this light-becoming that holds peace in its chest. Peace is our nature. Peace is our most natural way of being. Peace is what we are. All else is illusion. Peace is the love that animates us. Peace is in the living and the dying. When the last breath comes, always peace.

Where in your body is there not-peace? Find these aching dark spots and tend to them. Their tenderness asks for you. Sense them. They are whispering to you. Your body, as a fractal of the universe, speaks. Where there is darkness in you that needs tending, there is darkness in the farthest reaches of the galaxy that will feel your tenderness in response. Your body is a portal, a gateway to the beyond. Treat it with reverence. As the knots unravel further, you begin to feel the spaciousness of peace. Your face relaxes, your breath deepens.

We begin walking through a forest of depth and grace. In this place of moss and green and light filtered through the majesty of the tree, you cannot help but feel peace. The tortured soul can rest for a moment as the cries of your ancestors quiet. The ones in your family line are not your only ancestors. There are much more ancient lines, lines to the stars that walk with you. These star ancestors hold your peace dreams in their mouth, and when you are ready, they whisper to you prayers to recite. The ones that unlock the next step. Learn to listen to them. Let this be your practice.

There is nothing to think about. Just be. In the being is all the information you need. Remembering that this embodiment can sense and understand on so many levels, deeper than your mind. The chatter has been your greatest distraction. You can release it now. It is ready to be quiet.

> *What is mine to tend?*
> Let this be your sole prayer.

Its simplicity is grace. From this, the peace you seek will naturally well up, over, and out, spilling everywhere. Let the tenderness of that tending begin in your body. Each sip of water, each bite of sustenance feeds a deep soul-body that has been parched and starving despite your fullness. The frequency of your body is determined by the frequency of what it digests - thoughts, food, emotions, air. Choose wisely and with intention, and all of your life will shift and transform into a spiral of syntropic upwelling, an experience of radical joy.

The simplicity of peace needs very little to be full. It is breathed into life, and clean waters keep it thriving. Seek these. And where you find waters that have been deadened, clean them. This is a life's work in itself.

The waters are ready. The soils are ready. Our precious prayer of tending is waking them now. They feel our soft hands that touch their memory, and they swell with gratitude. The amplification of possibility comes when we work with Earth and show her our peaceful love, and it goes beyond anything we could have imagined before.

In the forgetting, I shrank, as I'm sure you have too. I shrank and contorted over and over to make myself fit into a sick and deadened world that was senseless to my soul. It felt like survival. In truth, it was a daily dying. *Today, I choose life.*

Forgive yourself for the transgression. The deep work of self-forgiveness is all part of the path. We are awakening together. This liberation is collective.

Peace is a portal of song and prayer, and all are welcome. In this soft stillness of peace, we will find our freedom. It was always there, locked in the crystal of our bone, trapped in the light of our fascia.

These parts of us also shrank. They closed to protect our peace from a world gone mad.

While you came here knowing of this madness, it was worse than you expected. But you came here anyway, and knowing this, you can still do what you came for. You are a bringer of peace. A reminder of futures past. You hold this sacred mission in every cell of your being.

This is why you are here right now, reading these words. This is why I am here right now, transmitting them to you. Across the time and space of my writing and your reading is the grace of forever. We were always woven.

Now we see the new thread becoming a tapestry of light. As the knots unwind, the new tapestry comes to form, and its majesty is astounding. This is what happens when we settle into one another. When we allow the trueness of our soul's essence to embody. All the hiding was part of feeling what it is to be human. You can forgive this. And forgive those who still hide in fear. Huddled deep within their embodiments, afraid to open these ancient eyes. You can be brave for them, too.

This is the becoming you have dreamed of.
It is real.
It is now.
It is the peace that has always been you.

How does this look, you ask? As simple as your prayer. That is all that is required. Let it fall from your lips, feel the softness as it is spoken.

What is mine to do?
What is mine to tend?

Gaia will answer in light and sound. She speaks in vibration and hum. Learn to see and hear her again. These languages of light and sound are ours. Open the ways for them to reach you, and open the ways for your imprisoned light to escape. This birth was but a sleep and a forgetting.

Coming through the portal of your mother's womb, you entered the matrix of flesh and bone for this embodied experience. You sat on a cloud with star elders, and you made the choice to come earthside. Embrace this being human as an emissary of the celestial beyonds. It was always meant to be joyful. It will be once again. This new and ancient Earth is ours. We make it each day with our agreements, we shape it each day in our soft prayers.

The simplicity: *What is mine to tend? What is mine to do?* Nothing more is needed than this prayer and the listening. Find the ways to clear your vessel so that the simplicity is a weightless sense of being. Clear your vessel to feel fully the grace of this lifetime that you chose. When you opened your eyes to this Earth, you straddled the worlds. You are still able to hold this place of connection. You can time travel and space travel to those parts of yourself that need your new tenderness. Hold them back to their light and watch your peace settle even deeper.

Offer your grace to the knotted threads. Pull softly and gently with no expectations. This is all that Earth asks of you. She will support and find the perfect pace. And know that this peace surpasses time. It is eternal, it is always here, it is always you. These words are your invitation to bring those tender places into light once again.

7

SACRAL

CREATION ON THE QUANTUM FIELD

The sacral chakra is the seat of our emotions as creative, living beings with an animate life-force. It is also the center of connection to the pure, innocent cosmos. Emotions are energy in motion, feeding potent information from the field of universal energy and light back into our biological beings to help us understand ourselves in this reality. The sacral chakra is related to our sacrum, and it informs our sexuality and connection to creation, the womb, the portal through which life manifests from pure energy into form. Sacral is to be sacred, and this is the place of sacred creation. The force through which all that is human becomes itself.

A woman's body is a portal to grace. Her womb is the most holy of human organs. It is the welcoming home of the new soul, courageously returning to Earth to embody flesh, blood, and bone, despite the knowing of the suffering on this plane at this time. Some souls live only in the womb for a short time, never fully embodying on the earth plane. Their karmic destiny is to experience the black holiness of water, womb, heartbeat, and sharing blood with their mother. That span of days or months, seeming so short from our limited understanding of time, is actually an eternity to that soul, full of all the experiences and lessons they needed in that lifetime. You can feel peace about the spirit babies that didn't come to be. They are with you always, no matter how their journey looked from the human perspective. It is holy and whole and perfect. Know this.

It is no wonder that the forces of fear and control have aimed to control, dominate, and oppress the womb space. The womb is the actual portal from the universe of energy to the density of Earth. Magic. Divine mystery. Incredible and profound.

Regret is a hungry ghost. Stalking our days and nights with what-ifs and could-have-beens. In these spaces of remembering darkness, we forget the truth of the memory. The truth is that memory is also a story we tell, and in the telling, we create the past. This is not to say that denial is the answer; there are reparations needed for patterns of pain and violence, there is always growth to be experienced, in the best of times, deliverance may be granted. And, in the midst of that swirling regret, the smoke of dark shame, there is also the story of your joy. There is also the story of your innocence.

I once held a spirit child in my womb, and fear whispered to me to release them back to spirit. I knew I had this power, so great was my understanding of the universe. It felt like the most kindness I could muster in that moment when my life partner held so much fear about stewarding the life of another child, and I knew that it might tear us apart. The realities of Earth's gravity and human conjecture had created confusion. An inability for my beloved to see the gift of this soul's grace to our constellation of beings. In the fear and uncertainty, I whispered my apologies. Apologies that pulsed and configured like fine dust in the dark of night, to speak to that soul in my womb, that soul that inhabited my field, waiting to arrive earthside. I whispered that this was not the time, I was not the vessel, we would not be their steward, and I expressed how sorry I was for that confusion. When the cells failed to form into a heart and small body, I was not surprised. We had spoken of this, this sweet soul and I.

We had come to a painful realization that it would not be our turn in this lifetime to experience Earth together. Makani is that wind that blows around me on soft days, and I can feel their presence even now. I saw them as two blue Morpho butterflies dancing by the waterfall, dappled in sun, whispering, "I will always love you." Releasing the tattered butterfly wing I had found into the water with some coarse, blessed salt. With the salt of my tears reminding me that Love is all there is. That we are always bound by this. That their spirit will always be bound with me.

I must release blame and accept this story of my life. I must. Must I? It has not been easy. And the release is not complete. Maybe it never will be. Is this the contour of regret? Maybe regret is the ever-present pockets between calm that gently hold sorrow in their curve and refuse to let it go. Maybe.

I feel the grief of that choice in my bones. Perhaps this was our soul pact. To experience the almost and the could-have-been. Perhaps that is what our souls had agreed to. I can never know exactly, I can only tell the story as I wish the past to become.

Tears grace my cheek and remind me that I am here. I am now. There is such sweetness in tears. Such gratitude in their slow cascade down a soft cheek. Information in the salts that informs me in this moment, on this skin that feels the aging of years. Tears know not of time and space. They are timeless in their healing. And what of innocence? You would have been six years old now, Makani. I can see you.

When I know this story through the lens of regret, I feel the pain of my own smallness, the sorrow of my capitulation to a world that seeks to contain joy. When I know this story through the lens of compassion, I see the beauty of my own kindness, the power of my connection to source, the trust that spirit and flesh don't have to entwine in order to experience one another. That this spirit child is with me always, and even so, in that story, I can find redemption. In that story, I can find peace.

"I think it is healing behavior, to look at something so broken and see the possibility and wholeness in it."

— ADRIENNE MAREE BROWN

Our bodies are what they do. Our bodies become our movements over time. Our movement congeals into form. The geometry of emotions becomes the forms, the postures our bodies take with other bodies, and with this programming, we become stuck. Stuck in postures of violence, hatred, fear.

In the turning of these times, we learn new geometries and allow our bodies new movements, new emotions, new ways of being together.

We are becoming nomadic, unhinged from our places of stuckness, mobile as bodies of change. As our bodies become nomadic again, they are made fugitive and seek rest. You can become an asylum for refugees of exhaustion. Where the weary forms can lie down, reconvene, and reconfigure. This transformation requires deep rest with soft focus. The kind of rest that hears the waters within. It is surprising how difficult this rest has become for bodies of modernity.

Bodies that find meaning in busyness, restless seekings for the somethings outside one's self that add value to what has been construed as a being without intrinsic meaning.

What happens to our bodies when we remember that their purpose is being embodied? That the simple being of love and peace is the most profound purpose?

That loving our water and talking to the plants is our life's work. That the busyness of high rises and shopping malls is a symptom of profound inadequacy placed in our consciousness by fear frequencies.

To feel insignificant is to "in-signifiy-*I-can't*". What if we signify, *I can*? That shift alone changes a lifetime. It changes a world.

We are world-changers. We are also exhausted. The Earth is exhausted. All her creatures are exhausted. The kind of rest our exhaustion calls for first requires a remembering that the flower blooms because it is beautiful to do so. Whether or not she is seen, she blooms. And when the bee comes to suckle her nectars, she finds joy in giving everything she is, knowing that she will receive nothing of that honey in return.

This kind of rest is for the weary souls who have been told they were meaningless. We swallow these lies early on as our eyes first learned to focus in a strange new existence. Lies that whisper *not enough, worthless, unlovable*. Whispers have a special way of seeping into our tissues and building a house. Their quietness hides a force that makes a life until one day you reawaken to the mystical, magical truth that you were always a flower, blooming *just because*.

As we learned busyness, we learned to make plans. Plans make us feel important. They are answers to a mystery that felt too vast to contain. Plans are answers to questions, inquiries that should have remained in the void.

In the inquiry, our bodies find life.

In the answer, they are deadened.

Remember this and pray every day with an inquiry as simple as, *How might I be of service today?*

There are mycorrhizal, subterranean depths beneath the facts of our doing, informing our movement from those soils of dense humus that hold the rich, dark, fungal life of the most alive assemblages. These rhizomatic algorithms speak the timid instructions for new expressions of ancient knowings.

It is the time for courage, now, as the tender tendrils reach above ground for the sun. There is water rushing in through the cracks. Water that holds the knowledge of life since Earth's formation. Water that animates and enlivens. In oxygen, in water, we find a new home.

Widen your awareness of what is and allow the fickle desires to flow in and out like the tides. Swim in their swirling waters, but don't get swept away. These desires have been set forth by the stars in service to collective liberation. They are destined to become the tidal wave that sweeps through. I have seen it in my dreams—wave upon wave washing through. Destruction is inevitable. Compassion is a choice.

Become your longing and let it burn you down, burn you clean. Find solace in ash. Taste it on your tongue and eat the dead. They have offered their burned bodies in a prayer of remembering and redemption. Find the trail to star-speak through this suffering and go there. Go there. Go there. It is our ultimate. It is the way.

True commitment can only ever be to the present moment. Anything else is a thief of her treasures. Full presence is all that is required to become human well.

Like the birds who sense sun, we receive information in every *now* moment. When we awaken once again to receive this constant blessing of Earth information, we will once again be free. Collective freedom is our nature. We are nature, who forgot herself in desire and in the ego's whisper. As the formless becomes form, we remember our vastness. In it, we become lost… and found. This is our promise.

We carry you. Let yourself be held. Let yourself remember Love's way into your heart. Let that way connect your heart to your crown. The seat of your regal nature as a being of light. Your form is bound-less and mirrored in every fractal of form. This paradox is everything.

You have come earthside through the star portal of womb space. Of Earth for Earth. You chose this coming. You chose this portal. All is perfect, even the suffering. Relax and release far enough to see.

Your body is a fractal resonance of the divine. And science is the floor of our understanding, not the ceiling.

Be troubled. Stay with it. Find the others and start creating truly embodied cultures. Cultures of care.

"You can see this time as an affliction or as an assignment."

— STEPHEN JENKINSON

Out of the dynamic, cosmic celebration, we were created. We are to become celebration and generosity, burst into self-awareness. What is the human for? The human is a space, an opening, a holding, a temple, the breath where consciousness celebrates its existence.

"Your life is a comedic, shamanic, creative act you are performing on yourself. You have to find your Godhood in the midst of the carnival of late-stage capitalism."

— ALNOOR LADHA

Consciousness is untethered from form as we move into this next phase of unfurling. The unity of thought and being, woven within Gaia, through all sentience. Cement removal, asphalt upheaval, to reveal the tender earth beneath. Seeds that have been lying dormant for generations, ready to put forth their splendor and celebrate life once again.

The fire at your sacral chakra is designed for burning and creation. To burn the fear and shame to ash for compost and creation. In this space of womb and life force, women's bodies are a portal to the cosmos. Pulling ready souls from the ether into biological form on Earth. The wild magic of this process holds the energy of a thousand suns as one cell turns to two, and from nothing creates life. You came from this magic. You are this magic. Remember yourself as the magic of god and, simultaneously, the humble drop in an ocean of being. When you can hold this paradox of your power, you become, once again, harmonious with all of Life.

The human capacity to experience emotion and imagine worlds is both our greatest strength and the shadow that has turned Earth into a wasteland. When we use the imagination to speak the languages of fear, domination, and control, we end up with systems like colonialism and neoliberal capitalism. Programs of domination, destruction, and extraction that serve a paltry few at the suffering of the many. Humans and nonhumans are sacrificed at the altar of profit and greed. This is only one way to dream the world.

As a species, we are fully responsible and captive to this nightmare. Which also means we are able to wake from it. Some of us bear a greater burden in the unraveling. For those with privileges to speak of it and dream from relative safety and abundance, we must dedicate ourselves to the collective liberation of those at the end of colonial and capital excess. The violence of this gluttony has created a veil of profound suffering on our temple planet, and the earth cries with us in grief. We must simultaneously bear witness and build the new.

The full capacity of your imagination is devoted to building worlds of liberation and love.

I wish to tend the ancient sites, Earth portals, places where the veil is very thin and fae folk still dare to dance.

Trust the choreography and wisdom of metamorphosis.
Dance with the rhythms of spirit.

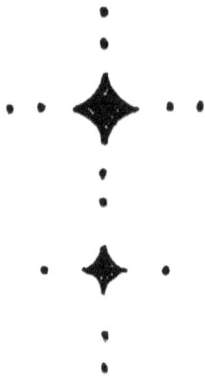

What are the architectures of peace for this time? When we unravel to be rewoven, what wants to emerge through us in the rebuilding? I embrace living with the wild rather than seeking to tame her. What wildness within you has been tamed beyond recognition?

Portals to the peace of source consciousness.
Connection with and feeling the inner body.
Presence in the now.
Cessation of thinking.
Surrender.

The essence of all things is space, emptiness. Silence and space are the font of peace. Become nomadic in the desert of finding yourself. Let the radical peace of this rooted search wander you across vast spaces, lit by starlight. In the patterns of the stars, find your story. It was always there. Feel the sand between your toes, warm from the sun of day. A million possibilities of renewal and remembering. Each one tenderly caressing your skin and mixing with your molecules.

Your co-creation with source requires a structure, a discipline, a shaping to bring it into form. This is why you came to Earth. To engage with her in this way, in this embodied form. What does this structure of your unique life's offering feel like for you? What are the body shapes and breath shapes that hold your creations? Tend those once you recognize them. They are the keys to the stories that want to become through you.

Discipline, rhythm, and routine that live in service to Earth are the sorcerer stones of a path to new worlds. With these curated and tender practices, you can build, shape, and grow the frequency of your creations. Tend to the roots and see the branches take shape like magic.

This is what it means to be truly radical.
The forgetting of humanness begins early.

With submission to parents, structures, and authorities, we navigate our way to what we believe is love, mistaken for survival. Doing and saying things that feel soul-wrong simply because *someone said so*. Quieting your deep knowing, intuitive brilliance, to fit the structures surrounding you when you awoke. You came here to pull these dying creations out by their roots. This is the radical in you. This is the sacred mission of your birth.

In our quest for the architectures of peace, we learn the quiet and persistent languages of beauty. There is an aesthetic unity underlying all the livingness of Earth. This is a collective language that has existed since the beginning of Earth herself. It is felt in the wild waters, the time of trees, the memory of stone. Our journey back to this wild weaving of beauty is a journey of healing the wounds of war. We heal the agony within that has felt the damage done to our mother. As we face this damage with courage, collectively, in our radical relating, pulling the wound at the root, we become the peace that is our most natural state of being. Facing the wound is both a personal and a planetary agony.

Facing it is the first step toward healing it. You came here to hold this. You remember. I remember.

Language shapes how we perceive and act in the world. Forming a rooted, radical element within that informs every aspect of our life experience. Our behavior, physiology, and personality transform in response to language. Oppressors understand this, which is why language is the first to go, the first to be controlled, when the oppression virus overtakes its host. Languages of beauty are the only truth of Earth.

Beauty shows us where we are on track and where beauty is marred, scarred, or lacking, and we know that we have strayed from our mother and her dreaming. Beauty is how we navigate Earth-speak to remember peace.

The blooming of a flower, sunlight dancing on water, the texture of soft grass on skin. These remind us of Earth's soul song. The black water that no longer gives life, the discarded human trash lining a beach, the smoke of toxic fires meeting air...these tell the tales of human forgetting. Learn to read these sacred texts. Translate their songs. They are the pathways to freedom and our collective liberation.

The circle is a primary architecture of peace. In circles, we remember wholeness. The power of the circle is that we open the sacred space in safety, to feel more fully the wound of this moment in our remembering of the holy wholeness. Once safely held to experience the grief, encircled, we can feel and alchemize it into new, life-centric ways of being in communion and community with Earth and her beings.

Touching the tender wound of this world, touching Earth at her softly beating heart, my own gentle heart needs holding. The circle catches this and soothes the loneliness of our fragmentation. Without the circle, we can succumb to overwhelm in the soul that feels like deep grief, but has no place for tending it.

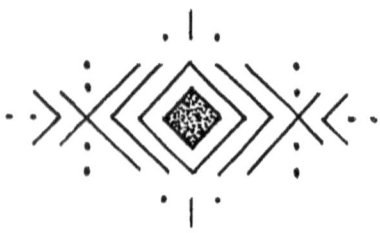

Wrapped in dragon,
white bear,
unicorn magic.
I am priestess of Gaia's goodness
shedding layer upon layer
of patterned pain.
Wounds of worlds and felled trees,
the numbness that laughs at suffering
as a sickened way to assuage the sadness
that overwhelms.
The goddess of Gaia whose heart beats with hers.
This goddess of Gaia whose heart beats with hers.
I am brave now to see,
Courageous to feel.
Supported in my divine role as shepherd of these
futures.
These futures of imaginal cells becoming one,
reunified as source wisdom.
Eyes upwards, white ceiling
fan slowly spins
the thought arises
simple and pure
we are the poem on the wind
carried forth by stardust
propelled by the sun
we are the wild life
we've been waiting for

unlocked
unleashed
single tear
washing cheek clean
we are the haphazard currents
more enmeshed than separate
we move,
touched by angels
whispers of spirit
whose language we are slowly
remembering...

8

SOLAR PLEXUS

THE FIRES ARE LIT - TENDING THE FLAMES OF YOUR POWER

The solar plexus chakra is a seat of life force energy. It feeds the stomach, liver, gallbladder, pancreas, spleen, and nervous system with energy and capacity. This chakra energetically feeds our intuition and connection to the universe. Our life's fire, the flame of aliveness, animates our bodies of stardust and water.

From here we find the sacred question: *What is ours to do?* It is ours to gather the sacred wood and light the holy fires. To tend the circles of creation and wash in the gentle flames without fear. I feel so much love coursing through my being. This love is entangled with my tears of grief. Grief and love are twin flames. We grieve that which we love. Love is a portal to grief. Feel it, my beloved. Feel it courageously. Your capacity to love grows with your capacity for grieving. Don't let your grief be stolen. It is holy, wholly sacred.

Peace seems impossible to a world at war. There are deep systems of war, violence, and hatred embedded into our biology with geometric, mathematical patterns that have been there for ages. We embody these patterns in shapes and postures that are below our seat of awareness. We cannot help it. We meet each other in these postures and perpetuate the energies of fear and violence.

The shift to peace requires new geometries, new systems written into our biology. You hold the merkabah awakening within. The sacred geometry wants to emerge in your being. Healing needs space and attention from you to open. Become an inner archaeologist. Tend to your own excavation. Excavate the war within yourself, scoop it tenderly from your being.

Where is violence embedded in your tissues? Where has it found hiding places to nest in your emotional histories, chemical processes lodged within the organs and cells of your embodiment? Seek these places through your breath and your remembering. Release and forgive.

Gently hold these places of war, of violence, and love them, unconditionally. Offer them back to where they came. Let them go. You have been holding a knife of fear, and it cuts you every time you use it. But you have been afraid to let it go. Not knowing who you would be without this. Let it go. Release. Remember.

Forgive. Integrate. Breathe. When you drop the knife, it transforms into light, and it goes everywhere.

Peace on Earth is possible.
In peace, I am free.
Breathe.

Listen now to the silence, it is the most potent carrier of presence. Eternity does not mean endless time, it is no time.

Silence and space are the font of peace. Our embodiments are eternity's way of experiencing time. When we tap into the silence, we remember our source code of eternity. Sometimes silence is trapped between sound, keep listening for the pause between. In this space is a vibration of profound love and pure acceptance. In this nectar you will find the rest you seek.

There are movements in our bodies that are invited to meet this moment on Earth. We feel off balance in our lives because of a distortion in the dominant culture that makes war of peace and violence of love. When we find the source of this distortion within our own embodiment, we have the capacity to shift back into our original blueprint, our divine design of peace and presence.

This design is Earth-print.

When we shift within, we become legible to Gaia once more, and in this language we are once again legible to our own soul. The seed of this shift is found in our belly, the root of this shift is found in the Earth.

"Quisieron enterrarnos, pero no sabían que éramos semillas. (They tried to bury us but they didn't know we were seeds)."

— *ZAPATISTAS*

Hua n. *Hawaiian for: fruit, tuber, egg, produce, yield, ovum, seed, grain, offspring*

> *Seed swimming*
> *Hua stuck to my skin-fur*
> *the moon on a rise*
> *wet with fingers to catch*
>   *the beginning*
>
> *slipped right by*
> *with the oils of forgetting*
> *but the hua remains*
>
> *slowly heating to bring life*
> *slowly releasing the hard cover*
> *the armor that shielded the soft*
>   *fruit, sweet and tender within.*
>
> *words that travel on the wind*
> *seeking places for planting*
> *the word that is the word that*

is the word ready to huli
to give of her essence
the package that is her beginning
a middle
and end
stuck in the movement of a world gone mad

she seeks the place of planting

where soils reek with compassion,
where winds blow with tenderness,
where disconnection comes undone.

I am confused in the certainty
sure of what is coming
confused about what has been.

graying temples speak to a blessed authenticity
that hid in the halls
of release.

pregnant hopes riddle a purple moon
she is sure of this forgetting
it is the only sureness of her fragile worry
supplicant essence...

we seek the percussion of a
        crinkle
                click
                        roll
to remind us, the drum hasn't stopped
        its beating
the band needs a leader
the audience
        a chair

where are the exits in case of fire anyways?
where are the worms who will crave this new food?
where are the beetles to craft a beginning?
where am I in the face of Pele's fire?

settling softly on the warm moonlit wind
hua falls gently to brown, dark earth
nestling in the hummus of life giving
　　　richness.

she softens
　　　and sighs
　　　and releases her riches
the softness of forgiveness
planted
the darkness of surrender
released

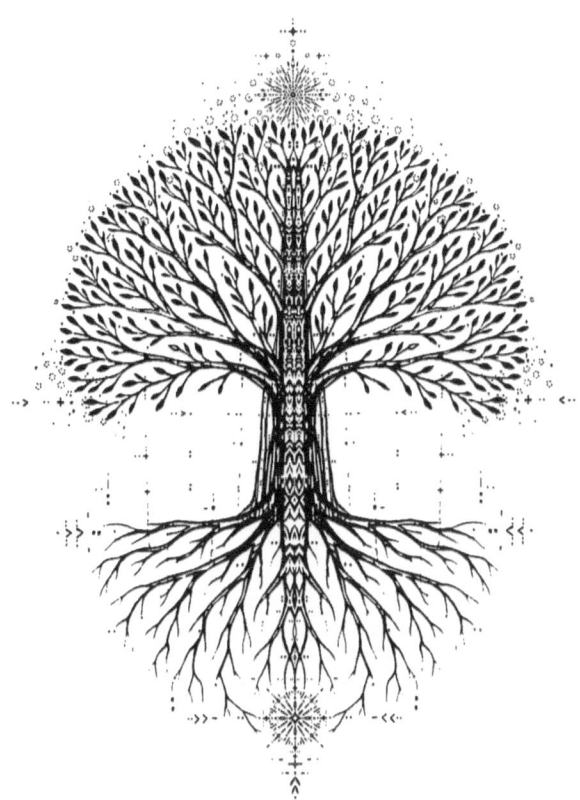

She stood at the edge of the grove, silent at the temple of roots. The banyans wrapping around stone, encasing the past with movements beyond time, slowly reminding the patterns of human imagination the reverence of their origins. How much of my old life do I carry into my new one?

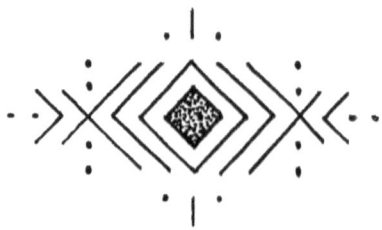

There is a light in my bones
Messages from a new and ancient world
That is already
And is waiting to be born
In the gestating,
All must come undone
This unraveling, untethering
will both pull at your heart
And explode it with wonder
Find the cave of your restoration
And rest there
There are sweet waters, wild, for you to drink.
Sleep with stars in your eyes
To feel the map of your destiny
It is a destination that has no arrival
A shape and a texture

You are both random and intended
A dance to be danced
A song to be sung
Make way fellow travelers
Breathe light into bone
Make way for this turning
You are magic embodied.

As we weave our ancestors' voices into new songs, the tapestry of peace becomes around us. When we begin to fully exist at these frequencies, new worlds of dimensionality open for us and we can float among the fears, invisible to their touch. This is the stuff of magic.

Salt is the crystalline memory of water. Water's words become form from the formless fluidity of its knowing. Each deposit melded with the particular earth it touches. Each deposit perfectly created to translate earth's daily message into our embodiments.

The ancient ones made ways to catch the water in rock, on wood, in vessels they made for this purpose. The salts precious and revered. The water within the human requires merging with these salts and through the gathering of salts, the ancients communicated with Gaia's waters, learning of places far away that traveled across oceans to speak to them in dreams. This is how we moved. This is how we learned of next steps and visions to propel us onwards in communion with earth.

Holding the potentiality of electricity, the potentiality of pure power, the salt crystals represent the potential of communication with the divine.

You are the brilliance of the sun herself, grounded as the Earth, your body lit with the love of a million fires. At your birth, more than 10,000 times the energy of the sun coalesced to make the supernova that became you in this human experience. Whole and holy. Wholesome.

The waters of your embodiment seek to understand the words of Earth's waters. The salts are the bridge between oceans' depths and the magic of your being. Thousands of miles these waters have traveled and being in the ocean they speak her entire language in one drop. Whale song and jellyfish dance, these waters hold and transmit the powerful energies of earth that you witness in waves.

Ingest of this deep earth wisdom and as the salts rejoin with the waters of your body. The electric pulse created connects you to the mother tongue. She is ready to speak through you. Feel her presence within. Begin your days this way, a glass of clean water, blessed with your intention, joined with salts of our ocean. Let these salts speak to you in silence and listen deeply for the day's message. Everything you need is there.

The relationship you have with water will nourish all aspects of your being. Speak to your waters, bless them, thank them, apologize to them. The world as it is built has ingrained harm into the waters because the fear frequencies understand water's power. Let your water soak in the moonlight and then drink of the moon's message. In the water is encoded a language that your body understands. Beyond the mind, it speaks to the multitude of beings that make up your embodiment.

They hum with these messages and bring your being into alignment. You are the gardener, the keeper of soil and soul. Making magic of sun, water and millions of allied beings. Your human circuitry is a system of empathy, representation and creation, designed to regulate and evoke biology. Feel the frequencies of creation and what they need in nurturance and nourishment in order to flourish and thrive.

You sing the songs that assist Gaia in maintaining her fertility of biology, a task she often has done alone. In spite of, rather than assisted by, humankind. In her aloneness she has cried for your remembering. Bringing all her voice to bear as she asks you to listen deeply once again. This co-creative possibility is the purpose of our birth into human beings.

Entering that beautiful flow with life brings meaning to the light of any morning and turns the daily rhythms of life from a mindless drone into an ecstatic dance.

Gratitude and attention are the only prayer needed. These simple acts create worlds where grace is possible.

We swim in a gorgeous mosaic of informational energies. The full maturity of your incarnation is the relaxing and healing of all the blocks that inhibit from this profound stream of communication. It is coming through and all around in forms of light, beauty, sound and frequency. Your mind tries to make meaning of this through the filter of language and ego. These are merely tools of human capacity, not its essence.

The solar plexus and the energetic bodies are a point of access to Gaian speak. Clear this portal to fully open with a pure channel and you will have access to the immensity of creation.

Do not be affected by the spell of materiality. Love and enjoy the world of matter without needing to possess it. The addiction to desire and its jealous modes of scarcity and protection feed the subtle bodies of greed, fear and shame within consciousness.

Experience materiality with the fully committed knowing of its impermanence. Impermanence and eternity sit in pure paradox. They are both true and both always.

When you embody the full presence of this paradox, you can release the grip of desire and enter a stream of experience that allows the full succulence of beauty to enter in a way that fulfills you instantly and absolves the need to possess and guard that which was never yours alone. Do not restrict the flows of materiality with your fears. Let the wealth, the true wealth, of the earth flow through you.

When you experience this fluidity you will understand the pain caused by our belief in scarcity. These are prisons of our own making. Become a conduit for resource to flow where it is needed. Give freely as a beloved passageway of matter and love.

We create prisons of our own making and then cry for freedom from within their walls. You are prison, guard and prisoner all in one. Rewrite your story to remember your freedom. It was, is, and always will be.

I believe that the future and past are embedded in the present. How we are, and the frequency of our inner experience in the present, is the future we will experience. That capitalism, imperialism, and colonialism are dead technologies. They are in hospice, and our best hope is a graceful dying. Trying to uphold them is pointless. Trying to fight them is unnecessary.

That the new worlds are here in the ashes of the old. As gardeners, we cultivate diversity and compost the old into the new. You are designed to be a co-creator with Life.

When we come from love and see through the eye of the heart, peace is possible. Love is our core strategy and tactic. Let love lead.

Peace will look nothing like the present. Allow the excitement about those futures to animate your dance in the present.

Letting go, trusting Life and surrendering to soul is the most important work you can do.

Relational, animate, loving, peaceful, compassionate and gentle are the invitation to peaceful, ecstatic futures.

"As a culture worker who belongs to an oppressed people my job is to make revolution irresistible."[1]

— TONI CADE BAMBARA

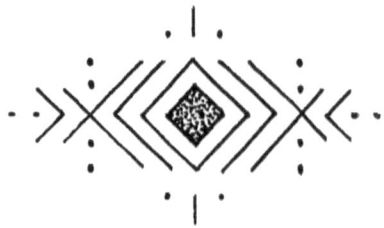

The prayer for listening...

Dearest Gaia,
my deepest prayers
to hear your song in fullness
to become the dreamer of your Dream.
May my being relax fully into surrender
may my heart open gently
to receive and offer only the truth of what IS.
I am a sacred warrior of Love's light.
May I attune to these precious frequencies
to digest my instructions
each day inhaling light's codes
of lifetime remembrance
until this prayer
becomes so interwoven with my being
a memory of starlight
shining as the sun
without effort
or explanation
eternal.

9

HEART

THE EYE OF THE HEART, A 12-PETALED LOTUS

The heart chakra is the center of our love and our will. Our etheric heart, the one made of frequency and love, is shaped as a 12-petaled lotus that encompasses the whole heart space of our chest. The eye of the heart sees truth. The Tree of Life grows here.

The biological heart sits within this energetic heart center and is an electromagnetic etheric antenna of sense-making that is more powerful than the organ of the mind.

"The heart connects us to the source of all in a field of energy that extends far beyond what we perceive as the borders of our skin. Our heart creates a powerful energy field known as a torus. The toroidal field extends far beyond the physical body and has an electromagnetic reach up to 100 times greater than the human brain."[1]

— BROOKE STUART, "ON THE TOROIDAL FIELD."

A horse's heart field stretches up to nine meters from their body.

Whales' and dolphins' heart fields vibrate and are amplified by water, reaching even farther. We are born with six of the petals of our heart lotus alive and aware. It is our life's work to awaken the other six, restoring our heart to the magnificence always available in its original design. This is what it means to awaken true sight. This is what it means to see through the eye of the heart.

The gospel of Mary Magdalene was found with the first six pages missing. Her gospel began on page seven, the number that guides our energetic system, the number of miracles.

She speaks of Nous, the vision, the sight that is the way of soul-seeing, the way that the heart sees. In wholeness and with a multidimensional awareness that dissolves old patterns of humanness. Patterns that were created from tattered, stained cloth. Patterns that were cut from the ways of domination and extraction. Patterns that have sought to defile Mother Earth.

Ascension is not a rising into spirit; it is a descent into the design of our embodiment, a descent deeper and deeper into the heart.

We descend and root. We remember and relax.
Rooted and remembered to Earth, we reconnect with our natural ways
of peace.

When we learn again to see through the eye of the heart, the whole world around us transforms and becomes achingly precious and alive. When we learn again to see through the eye of the heart, we can find eternity in a birdsong, and starlight in flower petals. The grass growing through concrete reminds us what is possible despite the seeming weight of the world. Love is the joy that is possible in every present moment as human beings. It is all within us, ready to be reawakened.

On this path of remembering, I have felt the flutter of the bird beings, waiting, shy, behind my shoulders. My wings beginning to form in their presence, I felt my spine straighten, and soft wings unfurl from my shoulder blades. Beings of light come to whisper truths in our ears. They come to remind us of our source, our creation, and our creator. We are peace-beings, most at home in harmony. We sense the day from wind and sunlight, tasting information on our sensitive tongue to know what today will bring. Our energy bodies feel the moon and the stars pulling gently at our waters within.

From this incredible display of beauty and information, we have all the language we need to know our next right step. When we align our intention with that of the dawn, we will always know which way to turn. The wind will tell us every time. The vibrations within our form are, themselves, frequencies of light. Always seeking harmony and peaceful tones.

Fear of the future is an introduction, not something natural to our being-ness. The natural feeling of fear from danger or immediate harm was a gift given to help us navigate embodiment. Fear of the futures, of something that does not yet exist, may never exist, and does not pose a threat, is not natural to our beings. The vibrations of this kind of fear run slow, heavy, sluggish. This kind of fear weighs us down as the mind takes over and runs worry through its pathways, creating a clog, a clot, a block within, which ego hides happily.

The energy of repetitive fear feeds the thought forms of domination and oppression. Domination and oppression are living beings of their own, and once they are loosed upon a mind, they replicate and amplify, creating a discord that is not native to our being. When whole collectives vibrate with this discord, it becomes harder and harder to hear the harmony of peaceful emergence. Bringing our peoples back to this remembering, back to the harmony that is our peaceful way, is the work of our lifetime. It is the reason you are here, reading these words now.

Even in the process of death and dying, there is always, at some point, a pure peace. Fear is a powerful tool, meant for embodied discernment to serve our peace, but it is not our master. In a world where fear reigns and replicates more of its own kind, our joyous work is that of peace. Peace-ways and peace-thoughts. Peace songs and peace movements. The vibration of peace brings the discord of fear back into harmony with the Earth—the way of the fully aligned heart.

I have found the seeds of war within me.
Seeded there by ancestors of fear.
It is up to me whether my soils support their blooming.

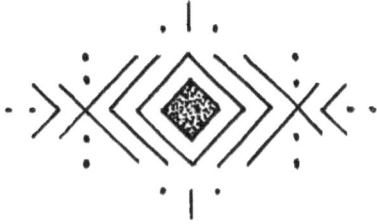

We will reweave the world in our voices
Making new myth that dances with the magic of Life
In this lifetime, what is the greatest service I can
    embody?
This begins within.

I am earth, mineral, blood, and bone,
elemental and cosmic all at the same time.
I am a miracle. I am magic.

We will reweave the world in our voices
To sing the myths that dance with the magic of life

I feel overwhelmed with the grace of this body vessel
that so faithfully carries me in this lifetime

We make medicine and miracles with the earth

Prayers replace plans
The question replaces the answer

Sitting in the not-knowing
we can become comfortable with the discomfort
necessary for healing

We prophet together

In community

Mahalo mahalo mahalo
Mahalo ke akua

You have been preparing for this your whole life. This is the time for miracles and crazy, wild synchronicities—the merry dance of unconventional being. You are becoming sane in an insane world. You can feel this in every fiber of your being. The confusion sets in when you listen to what the world wants you to think. These are the confessions of dying systems as they take their last, burning breaths. They will try to conjure fears in you, anxieties of the unknown. Push you to choose the devil you know over the unknown miracles that wait on the other side of courage. Do not be deceived.

Learn to speak the languages of fear so that you can translate and recode their meanings back to love, rather than being captured in their shallow trance. In the trance, you forget your distinctions and become the tone and tenor of mediocrity. That purgatory place where you live between fear of being fully seen and grief over the ways you hide your true self. This is a prison of your own making. You are at once the captor and the captured. And this means you alone can set yourself free.

Find the freedom-speak beneath the propagandas of fear. It is right there, just beneath the surface. And once seen, cannot be unseen. Find the courage of the heart to see and let your world as you've known it shatter. When the shards of that icy glass become a million pieces, the rainbow of your being is able to remember light again.

Killing another human is always insane. Even when that killing is in self-defense, the moment of destruction is a moment of insanity—a deep trauma for both the killer and the killed. There is never a justified death. Peace is the only sanity. Anything else is a lie, a justification, a forceful play by old systems desperate to hold their ground. What these systems haven't fully accepted yet is that their grounds are made of sand, and the ocean is rising to wash it all away.

The hardest and easiest thing in the world is to simply be yourself. When you lean into this divine design you chose when you came earthside, all the information you need is there. The rich contours of your uniqueness are completely ordinary. You don't need to worry about outshining others; we are all made of stars.

Your uniqueness is a gift that you live and give. And in the giving, you become receptive to the uniqueness of others, offering their being the permission to follow the path of sanity's wholesomeness. Get to know the contours of you. Face without fear your hurts, your mistakes, your guilt and shame. These are the blessed teachings you chose in the sacred contract of your life. You chose these teachings to etch the contours of your unique lifeprint deeper and more beautifully within.

The thing that hurt you most
becomes the thing that you can use to heal the world.

It is that simple and that profound. Look at those moments of your insanity, where you have learned to walk the ways of the world in its distortion, and then walk through the process of forgiveness.

In the indigenous Hawaiian culture, the practice of Ho'oponopono is an ancient practice to *make right* or to correct something that has created disturbance in the relational field. The core essence of this impulse is found in a simple prayer or mantra that holds the deep codes of right relation that Ho'oponopono tends. The phases of relational tending encoded into this practice are: acknowledging the wrong, asking for forgiveness, offering gratitude for the relational entanglement, and showing true and deep love for the other.

You can use this simple and profound prayer as a drumbeat, a mantra, a remembering. Where forgiveness and reparations are needed. For self, for other, for culture, for earth... Sing them, speak them, hum them. Offer them to your water before you drink. Your food before you eat. Your body as you wake each day.

I'm sorry
Please forgive me
Thank you
I love you

With these simple words, a cadence is created, and we can walk step by step back to our wholeness. It was always there waiting.

Softly, softly, the generous touch of wave sound in
*   white light room.*
Hand on heart and hand on womb, seeing infinity.
Circling between heart and creation's space, glowing
*   orange and green, endless energetic connection.*
You cannot have our fear.
In the face of the unraveling, joy has been given soil
*   and air to bloom with ravenous, unapologetic color.*
Clouds pass in silent witness to this poetry.

Clouds capture the essence of water's wisdom in ephemeral form. Making shapes and space to translate our dreams into vision. The ancients knew this and read clouds for their wisdom teachings. Clouds are an emissary of the Earth's moods translated into water language. You knew this as a child. Our forgetting is not anyone's fault. Forgive this, too.

Your heart knows the ways.

Declare yourself to this world. Don't hold back. All of you is required. All of you is loved. It feels very vulnerable to declare. Bold. How can I live up to this greatness? But you can, and you must, because you are already great. You are infinite.

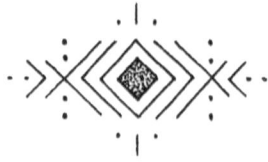

I will be good to my body and listen to her wisdom.

I will make space and quiet to hear my intuition, and when I hear it, I will trust it.

I will commit fully to my decisions and be completely honest with myself and others about what I can and cannot commit to.

I will make decisions with Gaia and Life at the center.

I will surrender to the flow of my life with full trust.

I will withhold judgment of others, embracing curiosity and empathy as my tools of right relation.

I will seek to fully comprehend and follow my life's dharma without comparing myself to others.

I will treat myself and others with the respect, gratitude, and admiration that is in accordance with our divine spark of life force.

From our place of wholeness, we can draw all the suffering inward.
Calm and silence the drama, the blame, the identification with the suffering.
Become an audience to your own fate.
Enter the sacred drift...

Ask yourself, and hold this inquiry as you move about your days: *Where in my life am I not free?*

"And our freedom depends on other people's freedom, for our fates are inextricably interwoven with others', especially with those we love."

— PETER LAMBORN WILSON, *SACRED DRIFT: ESSAYS ON THE MARGINS OF ISLAM*

Find that space and breathe into it, releasing light into the tightness of contraction. Freedom is always yours. The futures are inviting us in. They create themselves with the sanctity of our breath. We must pause to grieve. And then everything about our lives must change. Everything.

This is an invitation to joy, health, and prosperity. Do not be afraid. This is an invitation to our greatness. We get there through the embrace of our living as ceremonial beings on a divine temple planet. We get free together through the eye of the heart.

When the whole world becomes alive to our senses, freedom is the breath that breathes us back to wholeness. This is the initiation into life-as-ceremony. Where each mundane moment is an opportunity for the sublime. When we see the magnificence of this earth, we enter the realms of magic.

Let the darkness you find in those prisons of lifetimes be the edge that polishes the sharp truth of your light. Shadows contain mysterious miracles. We've been sold a lie about the devil of darkness. He is simply an angel cloaked in the black that holds all light frequencies. That darkness is the wisest of everything. There is nothing to fear there and everything to learn. As you integrate it all, your shine intensifies.

Your only assignment here in this Earth school is to love. The darkness knows this. There, you find the most love of all. Learn to love widely and wildly. Hold nothing back. May the sound of freedom's ring awaken you. You are nothing less than a sacred note, ever-lasting in the unimaginably precious song of the Earth.

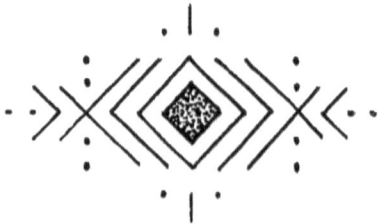

I have seen with my heart and felt with my eyes
I have smelled with my tongue and tasted with
my nose
I have listened with my gut
and dreamed futures with my ancestors' whispers

My roots have heard the call, mycelium running

When learning is decoupled from schooling
And we get clear about the difference

When passion and purpose are honored
No matter their uniqueness

When joy is the grade
No matter if we are legible to the markets

I have seen with my heart and felt with my eyes

The mother tree builds spirit within children
Remembering our greatness
Absolving our sorrows

We are goddesses and gods sleepwalking

Awake in amnesia
Rosemary gratitude scents us

Letters to the universe
in crystal and stone
Come yet, awaken with me.

A life lived in prayer. Living as ceremony. Meeting the miracle of your creation. Each day, the information is granted for the next right step. All you need to do is clear your vessel and pay attention. Beauty and suffering show the way.

We must collectively prepare to hold the grief of full awakening. It is the fear of witnessing the extent of what we have done that holds many back from waking within the dream. Compassion, grace, and the unconditional love of the mother create the conditions of possibility for the courage required to arise within each of us.

As I walk this path, I realize that my life is a consequence of my prayer. And I mean prayer in the most rooted, ephemeral way, as a thought alive with intention, a living moment of intentionality embedded within gratitude and surrender.

The primary process is the spiritual process. And we are simultaneously practicing embodiment in every moment. We are spirit incarnate in bodies. When we forget this and become obsessed with embodiment, we encounter and enact violence, despair, and fear. When we forget our body and become only obsessed with spirit, we become detached and indifferent.

Our belief in the individual, in the separation of the body as we experience it with skin and borders, is an illusion. You are a congress of beings; you have always been so much more than human. When you can soften into this multitude, you can relax the need to be perfect or good. Those judgments fall away, and the billions of beings with consciousness that inhabit you are allowed to speak. You can hear their whispers in dreams and breath. But only if you create the spiritual silence with which to listen.

When we become again, with the wholly animate world, and understand the wisdom of stone and the song of water, these dialogues are rich with information. Within that relationality, you can find the rest and nourishment you seek. The lonely deserts of separation have tricked us into believing we can only ever be parched. Within the interdependence and interbeing that have always been, you find yourself once again whole and at peace.

This is the age of consequence. Our ancestors knew of this unfolding and prepared us with story. We knew of this when we chose to come into embodiment at this time. Your life has prepared you to hold the grief of awakening. That is why you are here right now. There are no answers to guide us; seeking answers is what has led to our stuckness. Our desire to answer the question has allowed us to be controlled by fear. Our liberation exists in the inquiry.

When we seek answers as a salve of solidity, as a belief in safety, we begin the process of dying while still alive. Put your head to the soil and ask your heart for directions. The roots and mycelium speak in light and scent. Hold your spine straight and remember your star-speak. The dust of those ancestors will tickle your lungs with the information you need to serve the new beginnings. It will not come through thought in the way you are used to. Speak star and water and wind, and your heart will remember.

In this Great Turning, we witness death as we birth new worlds. It will take courage to ensure that our profound grief embeds within the new worlds as life force. We must ensure that fear, anger, and shame do not attach to our grief.

We must speak our truth - that love is the source from which grief finds its meaning. In this eternal understanding, the new forms are allowed to be clean, pure, untainted by trauma, free from the cycles of retribution and revenge, born wholly new and informed deeply by a loving vibration. This is crucial to the Turning.

Life changes inalterably in mere moments. It is so much easier to break than it is to build. We all carry the wounds of lifetimes in the very tissue of our being. And we have the tools and thoughts to shift these frequencies, to heal these patterns. Once healed, that vibration carries forward and backward for eternity. Your healing is food for the gods and ancestors. They seek your nourishment.

You are the future ancestor being dreamed of by those who will come after you. Time is not as we have been taught. You can time-travel to the parts of yourself that need your love. They are ready.

Invite the light of love to enter your heart center, to warm the loneliness of not-enough, to hold that sweet child of fear who stayed in her room for the protection and safety of smallness, the comfort of hiding. Invite her to expand, to spread like a mushroom sprouting in sunlit dew after a cold night. Riotous in her shape and announcement of being.

I wish to be soft to touch like this mushroom, spongy and forgiving. and connected to everything through the electrical pulses of soil. When I can stretch in this way and feel again the webbed endlessness of my being, I can quiet the old frequencies. They are merely a faint drumming of a past that once was. Not to be carried into the futures on my grief. Not to be witnessed in the now, where all of me is needed and welcomed. We who ride on the Turning, the time of great changes, the work of recalibration, retuning our divine instruments, are everything.

I am enough. You are, too. If I were not, I would not be here. *Enough* is the physical form itself. The encasement that allows a soul to dance. You were never just one anyway. All the beings that make you are bewildered by your belief in this not-enoughness. They lovingly wait for your clear vision to return. The whisper of not-enough is the distraction, the lie, meant to tame your greatness.

Enough is me. Enough is you. Magnificent is us.

"The slave ship never disappeared. They are not relics of a regrettable past, but active constituents in today's cross-world tensions and modes of becoming."[2]

— BAYO AKOMOLAFE, *"THE INVISIBLE CONSTITUENCY OF THE SLAVE SHIP."*

We wake up in a world gone mad and find forgiveness for our slumber. It was too hard to see this, the tender soul finding safety in numbness for a while. Until that encasement became too tight and awakening became her. She peeked out from behind the door of her safety and, one bit at a time, was able to take it all in.

This being human is difficult for the tender ones, even when we can remember our choosing to arrive. This is a time of witness. Witness and remembering. Maybe it was always this time. Now is definitely the time. When you find your center and the ways to nourish it, you become possible to bear witness, to see fully, and feel what is yours to feel. The fractals of suffering mirror each other. The patterns of pain vary in degree but not kind.

Witness is a noble path of service.

To understand heartbreak is to speak of dying, and to know forgiveness means to be reborn. No matter the circumstance. You can practice this every day. When you see the seasons change and Earth shows us her own practice of dying. Leaves change from bright green to vibrant red and then fall with grace. Fire sweeps old growth and creates ash for new beginnings. Flowers bloom with beauty and then die with softness. And when you live to witness the growth of Earth's spring, you understand these incredible turnings within your soul.

We once swam in rivers and climbed in trees without knowledge of steel and iron. The softness of the bark, the liquid of the water, blends with our beings and allows a much deeper communication to transpire. The creations of man's modern mind reflect a desire to close these portals of earth-speak. Perhaps the closing came from fear of the mystery. I sit still with a deep inquiry as to the origin of these thoughts. Thoughts that, at some point in our stories, took hold and became dominant. When we understand that wetiko, greed, hate, and violence are choices and we can begin to choose differently, the ripples of our effects radiate throughout the cosmos.

What is the shape and heft of your freedom ship? What songs are sung on its deck, what dreams are dreamed in its bedrooms? What new land do you sail for? To swim in these questions is to live a life of peacemaking. Freedom ships don't carry cannons. They bring seeds and poems to the newest of shores. When our earth becomes a freedom ship again, the love waiting to radiate from our hearts will know breath again. It can happen in an instant.

Make this your daily prayer: to be shown the next right step in your gloriously small life. The outsized nature of you rests in reveling in your smallness. This is the smallness of the drop that knows it is the ocean. Not the smallness of the fearful one.

In understanding your space, the space you take as one embodied being, you can rest in the fullness of your incarnation. It is here that your purpose will flower because it is tied to the wind and fueled by the sun and connected to an infinite number of other drops, other small space-takings that all weave a tapestry of such infinite beauty that your moments of comprehending it are what you call *bliss*, they are what you know as *God, Goddess, Great Spirit, Life-Force*.

What wood will you gather to build your ship of freedom? From which forests will it come? These are the questions I wish to have animating my days living with Earth. I am not *on* her, but *within* her now. Feeling her heart beat as mine. Allowing her breath to breathe through me and inform my next word, my next thought, my next dance. In this way, we repair the torn threads, and like magic, they reconnect. As the nodes of electric information come back online within our bodies, the same happens in the soil, and the same happens between us and our earth. She is so gracious to wait for these times. She has allowed us to experience our madness. And now she demands that we shift. Her patience is worn thin, and she holds us in fierce compassion. We must honor this.

It is safe to awaken. To open your eyes with new knowing. To see the insanity and your complicity within it. We will hold our grief together. It is safe to feel this. Grieving is your gift of love to that which was lost, that which was extracted and damaged. So that it may weave itself back into the tapestry of times. Feel this. We will hold you. It is safe to open your eyes and see. The absurdity of our mind's creations is coming to a turning. We will surrender iron and plastic for clean water and rich soil. Find the oppression virus that lives within you and know that attention is the antidote.

You don't need lofty degrees to do this—only love, water, and air. Love to hold the grieving. Living water to cleanse a parched soul and reanimate the earth's knowing. Air to breathe your prayers to the sun and moon. Anytime is perfect for beginning.

When we embody these teachings, we move through the eye of the heart. The eye of the heart sees in truth. You are here because you knew this. You spoke these vibrations in a space below thoughts, and it brought you here. I am grateful. I have prayed for your arrival. I have prayed for your reading of these words. Mahalo ke akua. It is safe here. Find your rest.

> *The subtle violences of colonialism and capitalism*
> > *whisper to us*
> *"faster"*
> *"not enough"*
> *and to these we say...*
> *I am the sweet wisdom of Gaia...*
> *I know my meaning...*
> *She unfolds with a soft and fluid pace...*
> *There is time enough for everything*

10

THROAT

THE SONG OF THE SIDHE - FIND YOUR FREQUENCY

The throat chakra vibrates with the speaking and receiving of our truth. This is the organ of our authenticity and integrity. The Sidhe, the Shining Ones, the ancient Elders who speak through these words, taught that we each have a unique note, a sound that is divinely unique in its exact frequency. And when we find this sound, this note, once again, the mysteries of nature open softly to us in our innocence.

In all things, pause. Slow down to hear your breath and feel your heart. Commit to the highest integrity and love for all involved and ask that there be no harm to Earth, humans, and all beings.

Lokah samastah sukhino bhvantu

You are a pulsing beat of energy being sung into existence in every moment. At any time, you can change this song and change your whole reality. Each song vibrates with the multitudes of others to create the reality we see around us. Your vibration has quantum effects. Never doubt your power.

The quantum field of energy, the collective field of our vibratory essences, this experience we call 'reality', is a dream. It is a holographic experience that we sing into existence. And we, the dreamers, bring it into being. Our collective dream has been distorted into a nightmare. With each breath of acknowledgement, each moment of grief, we dismantle and dissolve the forces that have held this nightmare in place. We can just as easily wake from this nightmare and dream peace. We can dream the peace realms into being. We can celebrate and dance our way back to peace. To freedom.

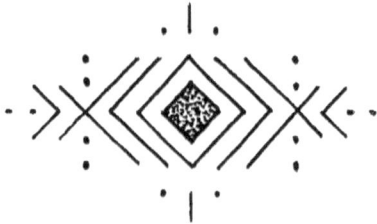

The peace of where the wild things roam
In my dreams
I dance on mountains
Where elephants roam
Eating honey
From the bees that cloak my skin
Their hum beat, my heart song

Where the owls tap my chest
With their beaks
And feathers line my skull

Where badger and muskrat
Finally make home together
After years of senseless wars

In these mountains, I dance
To remember my wholeness

Forgotten in Saran Wrap
On a lonely grocery store shelf
In that town we passed through last summer...
Was it Ohio?
Where fluorescents replaced the sun.

We went there by accident
On escape
It's all absurd
A carnival of sorts

Once we feared the dark woods
A place where witches roamed
Then I stopped in at her hovel
And went through the small door covered in vine
to introduce myself.
Smelled the herbs boiling in a pot
And let myself be served the healing tea
Prepared by her wrinkles
Soaking in love
And the wisdom of ancient moss

I don't fear the forest anymore
I see the carpeted hallway of my hotel
For what it really is
A pathway to dying in a body still breathing.

This is truth
I will face it with you

This peace I find
Where the wild things roam
This is truth.
I will breathe it with you.

In the mountains with stone and moss and badger and
    honey
And of course, the witches' tea,
It is here I will dance
It is here you can sing
It is here we can hold the world in our mouth
And taste its sweet essence
It is here we can breathe from the soles of our feet

It is here we can drink the secrets of silence

It is here we can drown in life once again.

May the peace of wild things make my life legible
    to the dreams of the waters
May the peace of wild things tune our tones to the
    cosmos
May the peace of wild things restore the wholeness of
    our holy,
pure innocence
As new becomings
Reborn.

"Gratitude is not just showing one's appreciation, it is the vocation of touching the conditions of our passing away."

— BAYO AKOMOLAFE

I am sitting with the hubris of things of grandeur. Imaginaries that say I must change the whole world alone. The distraction provided by a belief that we must change any world other than our own. The lie that it is even possible to do anything of meaning without first cleansing our own inner condition.

As human beings, we must stay close to Earth, air, and water. Stay close to nature and clean our vessel, physically, as well as energetically, and spiritually. From this place of pristine authenticity, it is yours to speak truth from the sensing mechanism of your heart. What will be, will be.

You don't actually have to do anything other than listen and follow the instructions for the next right step.

We came from pasts where every object, every stone, every plant, tree, animal, cloud was imbued with the life force of sacredness. These futures lie in patient wait, a wait outside of time. The rocks know a different sort of time, a patient, timeless time that doesn't bow to the ticking clock. The clock was invented to steal our timelessness, to steal the sacred drift that enabled us to feel Earth time, wind time, and water time.

When we moved with Earth time, we felt her rhythms and could speak to the stars. Once we embraced the clock, its tick-tick-tick creating a false beat, out of time with Earth. We began to measure time in human terms. We began to take time, give our time, waste our time, and feel that we had run out of time. We turned on lights at night to create more time, and we forgot the moon. Time became scarce and elusive. And this new anxious belief in time running out led us to forget our ancient roots. To believe that we only live once. To forget the miracle of our soul.

Remember, now, that we are timeless beings. You are always, ever now, being. Timeless in your eternity. Time-bound in a sacred body temple. Gifted the blessed experience of living within an earth suit, a glorious soft encasement made of billions upon billions of animate beings all working together to create you in every moment. Bacteria, viruses, protists, fungi, alive within and with you, communicating ceaselessly in a divine concert with your tissues and cells, with the water that flows through your blood, and the proteins that make up your muscular form.

You are a work of art, mysterious and inestimable.

These beings do this without thought of return. It is a gift. Priceless. In every moment, a gift. This beauty will stop you in your tracks. It is unfathomable and profound.

Speak kindly to these beings who inhabit you. You are like a tree or a bird or a dolphin or a whale, a divine form dreamt by creation, dreaming yourself together with the multitudes every single moment. They ask nothing and give everything. Your joy, your attention to their grace, is the ingredient of miracles. Sing to your body, sing to the innumerable lives that lend themselves to your life. Vibrate them with your love and watch the miracle of your being expand. Then you will remember that our myths of heaven are here, on Earth.

The sacred lives in everything. This remembering is what changes worlds. We have landed in this lifetime in an operating system grounded in separation, materialism, and rationalism. These spin and feed our fears. Our fears spin and feed these operating principles. The spiral, when unchecked, deepens dis-ease.

The courage of awakening within the dream requires holding the untold grief of accountability. I am here to hold your precious courage as you open your ancient eyes. Your song, the one from the Sidhe, will hold your heart open as you metabolize this grief. We sing together. Our chorus is unstoppable. Our harmony is profound.

Your life is a consequence of your prayer. The quality and impeccability of your prayer builds the sacred structure of your futures. The primary process is the spiritual process. You are a body inhabiting a soul. This body is a congress of beings, all originating from Gaia and oriented to love as a strategy and grounding principle. The substrate of your biology emerged through sacred geometries that made your human form. This is an endless series of miracles. Clear the space in your throat that has been blocked for lifetimes, and simply speak your truth. It is cosmic in origin and laced with codes of coherence. You can trust it.

You have always been more than human. You have always been a sacred phenomenon. Miraculous. The confusion that has left you feeling incapable, not enough, is stuck in your throat. Blocking the flow of aliveness and truth that is waiting to issue forth, bringing your world into impeccable coherence.

When you become again, in dialogue with the animate world around you, when every rock, chair, cloud, bird, and whisper becomes alive again, you remember your sacredness. It was always there. Always you.

In these dying times, love is the knowing. The way we love will allow death to kneel and give of itself. With love, we find Earth's time again in our cells and joy in our breath. We feel the beat of her resonance deep within her core, how it guides us. We remember the moon's pace and the star-speak. With love at our center, we become impermeable to fear, and we can move with grace and compassion even in cacophony.

Our peace is not without suffering. It is not ours to imagine a world of perfection or utopia. Utopia is the "no-place" that holds its own violence in the denial of suffering. Rather, our peace is one that tends to suffering with kindness. That understands the work being done with us as we move through the oceanic emotions of time and space, and experience the density of suffering with Earth. We metabolize the cosmos through our emotions. This is powerful, potent human work.

Our suffering is sacred, too. It is a blessed and beautiful part of this *being human.* This is a passage, not to be missed or replaced with saccharine imitations of joy. The sweetness of connection in a world where impermanence and imperfection exist, this is the nectar. Don't miss it in your quest for perfection.

You have mistaken perfection for self-worth in the course of your wounding. I am here to remind you that you came here to learn. You will never be perfect; it is a distraction built to keep you in fear, under control. When you dislodge the knots in your throat, the power of air and prayer rushing through you is like a tidal wave, bringing aliveness and balance, coherence and calm. Our truth is revolutionary in its kindness and courage.

These are times of collective liberation, and in the breaking of cages, there is a positive destruction. The force of Kali, Pele, goddess of fire, mother of dark birth, the one who remakes the world; she is with us now. We break cages of fear and burn violent systems with our songs of peace. These songs emerge from our healed throats without effort. Their fire in our being feels like water. Nourishing and silky. Fluid and fierce.

In burning back that which has become oppressive, addicted to dominance, fed by fear and violence, we turn these things into ash for the phoenix to rise. The ash is full of minerals for the new soils of peace. Do not be afraid of this process; you can prepare and be ready to ride through it. On the other side is the peace I speak of. It is waiting for you.

The new ancient futures are lands we travel *with* rather than *to.* They are *becomings, just* as we are becomings. They are songs to be sung and art to be witnessed.

Ideas are born through us to bring these new dawns. When you sit with your practices of perfection, your words of harm within that tell you *not enough, unworthy,* and *shameful,* when you begin to hear these as the wounded child of modernity herself, you can forgive the practices and systems that created her. Inside forgiveness is the activation of compost. And inside the compost is the new peace, waiting to be birthed. The soils are ready for this flowering. Our ancestors lovingly prepared them.

Our addiction to violence and separation within our minds and in the world is an unconscious infection, transmitted from host to host. It can be cured. What excavations do you need to do within your soulscape? How are you listening to the freedom song building in your throat? The one that finds frequency with the song of your birth. You were designed to perceive this turning. Awakening to it is natural, easy, full of grace.

How might we be precise rather than perfect? Precision is the gift of perceiving the fullness of Life in all its magic. Impeccability finds its roots in integrity and authenticity. In this way, language becomes pure, wholesome, and precise. Like poetry or art. You expose your heart and face the fears of humiliation, but there is no going back.

You will begin to feel yourself taken over by a higher self that was always there, lying in patient wait for your eyes to open again. Your words and songs will take on a potent power in their simplicity and searing truth. You will reach through the ethers of time and touch other hearts, exploding theirs with yours, awakening this new peace. Others are beginning to sing with you in a beloved chorus. This song is unstoppable.

There is an exact linguistic science of enlightenment. A spelling of the futures of love. Mary Magdalene knew this and spoke with the reverence of each moment. She is here within you. Hear her whispering. Every cell within the universe is a divine word waiting to be spoken.

"That is why the Good came into your midst, to the essence of every nature in order to restore it to its root."

— THE GOSPEL OF MARY

The etymology of the word *radical* is "to the root." When we remember that to be radical means to heal at the root, our movement can come from a place of deep grounding in Earth's knowledge. Magdalene's vision, her clarity of knowing why we are here. Become the radical who gets to the root and restores its life force. There is nothing to destroy, only soil to nurture as it feeds these new roots of peaceful futures. The composting of violences brings the ash that will feed your peace.

You must empty your cup so you can fill it again with the people, places, and ways that support you in the fullest expression of your Love.

There was something I needed to do...
There is nothing I needed to do...
The divine laziness of surrender takes hold...
I let Life lead.

Goddess of Gaia
I am dreamer, awake
shepherdess to new worlds
alive to the process
through me, all is potential

"Do not dwell in the *past, do not* dream of the future, concentrate the mind on the present moment."

— BUDDHA

How might you sculpt your living prayer into the divine alignment of your soulprint? Your causal body came with a light that is yours and is imprinted with your divine uniqueness. There is only one of you in all creation. Sit with that magnificence and be humbled by its ordinariness.

As you shed vestiges of the old in favor of this divine assignment, lean into the lessons of your suffering. You chose these; you are not victim to them. Only if you perceive your status as a victim will you become victimized. This is a hard truth to swallow. It often gets stuck in the throat. Sing your way through. Use whale song or bamboo breeze to dislodge it. Your freedom depends on this passageway clearing.

Digesting the shame and blame and returning to frequencies of wholeness. You are wholesome in all ways and always. That is the truth of your innocence. No matter what has been done to you, redemption, peace, and love are always, always available. No matter what has been done to you. Make this your prayer each morning, to release shame and guilt and inhale forgiveness. That Gaia reminds you of your grace, the grace that is woven into every bit of your being. The grace and the innocence that can never be fully taken from you and can always, in a flash of insight, be restored.

You have this power.
You have this power.

Expand into the fulfillment and understanding of these truths. Relax into the field of love that surrounds you. You have no calling or task that is more important than this. To be born again in God/Goddess/Great Spirit is to awaken to the Love that motivates and animates the sun, moon, stars, and all living beings.

What does it look like to be fully human in the dying times, in a vessel that is always dying and being reborn? Forgive yourself when you finally see with searing clarity all that you have laid to waste by giving up your sovereignty and surrendering to the whipping wounds of a thousand cuts from modernity's distortion. It is distorted and absurd what we do to ourselves, to each other, to life. Forgive yourself. We can hold this grief. Together, we can hold it.

Life will ask, *What do you believe?* Accept this challenge of integration and articulation.

With my full presence and when I embrace the practices that center this physical vessel in its multidimensional intelligence, heaven on earth becomes possible through me. When I become saturated with the courage to sing my authentic note, the clearing of my throat allows Earth to sing through me.

This will require the grace of our grief. The searing sadness of how distorted we have become. This will require fierce, terrifying courage. It will require standing up and standing out. It will take nothing less than our whole being.

Make your daily prayer one of commitment to the futures of life:

I am ready. My whole life has prepared me for this. I must tell the dying stories into the next world, alchemizing and composting their violence, so that stories of peace may awaken and shine. I must shed the guilt and shame of my privilege so that I may speak with confident humility and listen with full presence of heart and na'au, my gut. I must forgive and clear the passage of my throat to sing these songs of peace, the songs of Earth.

As the stories die, we must receive their final teaching, their full distortion and absurdity. Then, and only then, can we release them back to the wholesome blackness of pure creation. Rebirthing. Reborn.

11

THIRD EYE

CRYSTALLINE COMMUNICATION -
QUANTUM ETHICS OF CREATION

The third eye chakra is a portal of our sight, our understanding, and our entryway for ideas to enter our biological system. Ideas are animate beings, come to be born through us, the human is their main gateway to arrive and hold influence on Earth. The crystals at our third eye are birthing grounds for ideas.

An idea will move through the ethers, searching for its host, dropping in and visiting different human beings until there is one who decides to commit and give it a home. These ideas pulse from the center of the Earth and the vast space of the cosmos, from all the star nations and the ancestors past and future. They are coded with creation-speak, desire, and fulfillment. They are the spark of creation and evolution. The human being is the bridge to receive ideas, to house these animate beings, and to birth them through the power of our imagination and emotion. This is miraculous. Creation is who we are.

Through the third eye, we sense the quantum aspects of our reality that are below the other senses. In this way, we connect to eternity. It is no wonder that modern systems of domination and control seek to calcify, toxify, and numb this divine agent of insight. The third eye is a superpower of being human. If it has become deadened within you, know that you are not alone and that you can begin to bring this blessed center back to life. It is never too late.

The third eye holds and shapes our ethics, our understanding of right relations. In these times of radical creation, we inhabit the borderlands where the old crumbles and the new is being born. This is where ethics take on a quantum shape, an aliveness. It is the place where monsters and miracles are born. In transitions, ethics necessarily shift and form in emergence with every moment. What is right relation one moment becomes repugnant the next—miracle to monster. If you are not grounded, this will be disorienting and panic-inducing. And our ethics must be flexible enough, supple enough, to twist and bend without breaking.

The ability to ride the massive waves of change gracefully is fueled by our capacity for forgiveness and deep listening. These are times for reading the signs on the water and moving in concert with the energy pulsing through the waves.

We cannot avoid complicity with the toxic systems of culture that are alive in the moment. We are so deeply enmeshed in this dominant culture, physically, emotionally, in our dreams, in our tissues: the only way out is through. These pathways require daily forgiveness and the devotion of practice. Quantum ethics and deep grounding. Sensing through the third eye, seeing through the heart, knowing from the gut, and deepening our roots into the Earth. Our complicity is baked into the moment; we are fully entangled with modernity.

There is no way to avoid the suffering caused by your being alive in the world as it is. Don't dwell in guilt. It has been used as a tool of fear to freeze you and incapacitate you. Your guilt is a powerful sensing mechanism. Use it as a compass to see the boundaries of your ethics and where you have crossed them by the sheer act of being alive right now. Then forgive yourself, recalibrate, and move again in deeper commitment to the futures you can smell.

This is what I mean by quantum ethics. In constantly noticing where we have strayed, then forgiving and then sensing again, we move like a wave towards new worlds previously unimaginable. Like a wave that is unstoppable in its ability to dissolve the old and make way for something different to emerge, these new worlds also constantly move, shift, and shape. And as you move with them, you actively build the etheric shape of cultures and systems that will become physical over time. Trust in the work of the ether. See the scaffolding of future-culture with your third eye. It's shape is frequency and tone.

You become the animate bridge from now to the futures.

Your body, the rainbow bridge, is alive with energy and information from the universe, sourced through your chakras, the portals of energy sensing and sourcing that are the etheric body of your divine design.

You begin to navigate your ethics in an alive way.
Recalibrate in each moment, to understand the shifting sands beneath. It is the only way.

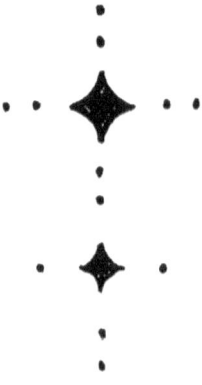

Your third eye is the portal to etheric realms of information. The world will try to calcify and dull its capacity with chemicals in food, polluted water, scattered thoughts, frantic energies, excessive busyness, lack of sleep, electric frequencies, and collective fear and anxiety. This is all designed to stop the revolution that is coming. A revolution of Love. It cannot be stopped.

You are part of this wave. It is building and moving along the frequencies of cosmic energies too big to easily perceive. They hold shapes that we move within and they carry us forward. You can trust this.

A human baby first forms in the womb of their mother as an etheric body of energy. On this etheric energy body, the physical form begins to take shape. Cosmic information moves through portals of sacred geometry using biological substrate to become physical matter as cells, organs, tissues, the body attaching to the etheric body through frequency and emotion.

The work we do in the ethers, the quantum, is profound and foundational. We are energy first. The density of physical form comes after and is shaped by the energy that holds its futures. All of this is made of Earth and stars.

In the same way that a baby forms in the womb, we collectively build the cultures and futures of shared dreams, first, as etheric energy formed from our thoughts and beliefs. Upon these thoughts and beliefs, the dream, the quantum, the physical begins to take shape. You cannot build only from what you know, or we will repeat in an endless loop the geometric forms of violence and separation currently programmed into our biology. These mathematical equations that determine our physical form were placed there by thought forms that intentionally built etheric bodies of fear. It is our work now to untangle and rewrite those codes.

These new bodies, ours and Earth's, are made of Love. You must build from the energetic frequency of what is not fully formed yet. Build from the peace-dream, surrendered to the frequency of Love. The only way to do this is to surrender to the impossible. The seemingly impossible is where the futures lie—peace on Earth.

Hate rides on the frequency of transference. It is looking for a ready and willing wound, and then it will leap. To the healing-healed being, it cannot attach.

Peace rides on the frequency of resonance. It softly rides waves of light and radiates into the core of beings in its presence. With power, not force.

Peace frequencies interrupt the transference of hate. Hate cannot flow in the presence of peace resonance. Hold resonance of peace within, and you will affect peace without. Effortlessly. The more who do this, the greater our shared peace and the less space for hate to find its woundings.

How, then, do we become fully human?
We love ourselves into the truth of who we are.

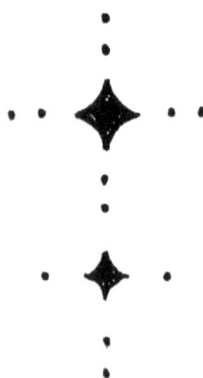

Our flesh bodies are quantum biological miracles of light, vibration, and love. Study your own biology, and this truth is everywhere.

When we alight the love that powers this magic, we become again the beings of peace that we always have been.

Shedding the layers of fear that hold us in beliefs of scarcity and lack, we find the frequency of the miraculous that enables us to speak the language of stars. The crystals in our third eye know how to do this.

Our roots are thirsty for the truth-speak of Earth's message. Our mother is unconditional in her love of our frailty. Embracing our sacred fragility, we allow Earth to experience herself and for this she holds us in pure loving grace. When we can know this humility deeply, a light is released through our being that radiates the experience of what myths call *heaven*. It has always been here. On Earth. In us. In all of us. Human and non-human kin.

That which seems without life is full of heaven. When you have the eyes to see and the heart to feel again, the entire universe becomes alive with you. In this flow of deep aliveness, joy is a given.

I touch the bark of this beautiful banyan, the temple beneath her roots, complete. The soft fires of forgiveness lit within her roots stretch from heaven's air to touch Earth's soil in a sacred entanglement. She, like me, is a bridge. Heaven to earth and earth to heaven, entangled. Growing thick and strong from the connection of soil to star, she shows me the expanding and woven embrace that is all of us. Always and ever.

Everything must change.
Everything always does.

I am an emanation of Gaia's grace
fully present
in the presencing of her dream
the futures' beauty
and the salinity of masterful creation
there is no playing small anymore
your breath will change the energies of a room
as you walk, the perfumes of truth make way
the lights turn on, the hearts explode
and all is at once abundantly right with the world
exactly as it is...

Of the dynamic, cosmic celebration, we were created. We are to become celebration and generosity, burst into self-awareness. The human is a space, an opening, a holding, a temple—the breath where the universe celebrates its existence.

Fear is a resonance, a frequency, and once you find the spine of Love in your being, you will become invisible to it. In this way, you remember your place among the immortals.

Technologies of sound, frequencies, have been lost to time. In this age, we remember their potency. Song, sound, wind, the frequency of fabric and food, the love with which you do the things you do in a day; all of these carry a frequency that is transmitted. Clean and clear your antennae to sing the songs of *ancient forever*.

I of the ancients,
skin of bark
blood of sap
I see the worlds that once were
and ever shall be
gathering in circle

technologies of sound
we are seen once again

Held in sacred
I touch Earth and she fills me.
ancestral knowing
traversing realms
I become disoriented
and must remember the ways

The only way out is through

Arm in arm
Star to star
Song in song
Whispering

I perform this for no one
And in service to all

12

THE CROWN

OUR PATH TO THE STARS

Humans are designed to be the bridge from heaven to Earth, Earth to heaven. Receive from the stars and pull that wisdom through to the radical root and into the earth. Offer up the soul of soil from Earth to the stars. Earth is sense-making through you and listening to her star ancestors with you. You are the bridge between these worlds. Use your natural translation skills to speak star to earth.

Relaxing at the crown requires surrender, trust. This is a daily practice. Surrender happens in the small moments, when life's littlest expectations are laid down in the lap of trust and release. Your mind races with strange, small thoughts... *I should have turned left. I wish the coffee was hotter. If I had gotten that sandwich, I would feel satisfied...* These persistent thieves of presence make way for their grander, denser kin... *I should have gotten that degree...moved last year... married that other person...* all the stories we tell are fictions of control that steal our hearts and distract our minds from the grandeur of the present all around us.

Restless and antsy, wishing for something other than now, the affliction of agitation is a faithful companion. Only full and embodied trust in Life herself salves this aching. Sovereignty is surrender. The flowers know this. When they open their blossoms, unafraid, wild beauty, sweet fragrances offered wholly to the world, they know that they will be picked and prodded and used to bring more life. This sacred duty is their gift of surrender.

In tune with the mother herself, a flower's life pulses with presence and beauty, rejoicing in this purpose. What might it feel like for you to be this wholesome? For your work and life to be lush with ease and nourishment. Marked by rhythms entrained to Earth, trusting the flow of seasons, wind, tide, sun, and moon.

We have too long been confused. When we realize we are One, we once again know that to surrender is to return to source, to return to Self, to guide ourselves deep into the mystery of our only one true home within. Here, anyone can live free.

Regret is a constant companion of this human-ing
the hungry ghost that feeds my fears
stealing my presence
with what-ifs and should-haves
if-onlys and whys

Regret is this soft sadness
that doesn't ask for tending,
only witness and the gratitude of presence

I wish to move with the deep purpose
of intention
intuition
and remembrance.

I have become dull to the signs again
time to sharpen my senses
clear the cobwebs of false truths
return again to the eye of the heart
and see clearly

informed by the love of a bee for his pollen
his life devoted to sweetness
nothing more
nothing less

A love note to the star beings, keepers of existence.. as above, so below...

Just as our root chakra opens to our Earth mother, the crown chakra is opened up to our celestial homes of wisdom and gnosis. Connecting back to the stars, the energy center of our crown is the seat of divine gnosis, the knowing that surpasses understanding. From the root in Earth to this root in our celestial star ancestry, we, the humans, are a rainbow bridge. We are magic. We are becoming.

We are stuff of stars
Bodies made of liquid light
And crystal stardust
The light that shines from within
A beauty that cannot be held
Only witnessed
And blessed
For a moment of presence
In that explosion of remembrance
The energy of a thousand suns...

All we have been told is a dream
From which

We are waking.
Remembering
There is only the way forward
Welcome to these futures
Where love is our language
Light is our nurturance

Today, the sadness, depression, and despair seep in through cracks, and despite the sunlight, I feel their gravity. Disconnected and lost in the middle of a crowd. Isolated, faceless, nameless, rudderless. Where is the moon? This place is beautiful and feels so empty. Devoid of joy. Missing a frequency and energetic texture. I see the birds fly by, seeking places to land on this perfect lawn of man-made grass. This soul longs for the wild, overgrown, messy places of creation. Where uncertainty and mystery foment and tangle.

When your energy is thrown, and you feel this texture of despair, find your roots. Deep roots that are in Earth. The ones that tend the dark places of magic and nourishment. Where nutrients are ready to love your despair into wholeness. You also have roots to the cosmos, stretching up from the crown of your being to touch star knowledge in the luminous expanse where ideas and inspiration speak.

What would it look like to embrace the flows of dense sadness, not as something to fix, but as energies to ride? Full, rich, and alive with potent information. What might this wave teach me about myself? About the universe? About the beings within me and their needs, their voices? Just feel. Just feel.

There is a place too for sadness, grief, despair, longing. These, too, can sit in the sun and remember. They are also a beloved piece of the wheel of creation, the wheel of emotion. This gift of feeling is an intrinsic miracle of the human becoming.

The bird who lands on the lemon tree clicks to remind me that they will come anyway. Bring even a bit of earth and they will come. The birds will not land for long on the manmade grass that is ever-green and plastic; they will not be fooled. But they will come for the grass that grows between the cracks, persistent and proud of its connection to the soils beneath. To let Earth know they see her reaching. The birds. They celebrate her resilience.

Life always finds a way to push through, with love and kindness, reminding us of what lies beneath the surface of our forgetting. All of these emotions point the way to new lands. Simmer in their essence and know that this too shall pass. It always does. All of us are wayfinding. Just take a step on your journey, each day, deeper into Love.

Being of star, descended to earth-gravity, you will often feel a heavy longing. You will feel lost. The disorientation is your soul-compass, to remember the portals of connection—the rainbow bridge of an energy body that is your guide.

Open at the crown, in a place where the skull stays soft at first when we are born, honoring the connection, giving us time to adjust to the gravity of our body. The calcification of bone over this portal cements a momentary forgetting. With new cultures of our ancient futures, this connection does not have to solidify. We can maintain our bond to the stars with myth, song, and our wholeness. We can remember that the density of bone also conducts light, and in this transmission of aliveness, an electromagnetic dance moves thought and inspiration between star ancestors and earth soil.

We are that bridge. Heaven to Earth. Earth to Heaven. Pulsing with frequencies of light in every part of our being. The eyes to see are yours. With this work, you reawaken them.

I am navigator
Wayfinder
Sister to the stars
Tethered to the moon
Guardian of stardust and angels
Incarnate and precious
I dream futures into being.

Holding your hand
Eyes-a-twinkle
We head home...

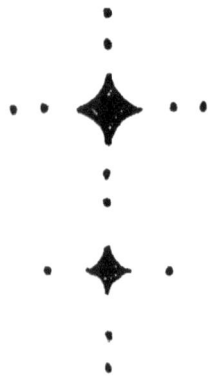

13

CLOSING THE CIRCLE

OUR BELOVED FUTURES OF INTERBEING

L et your soul expand to meet your skin and feel the world in her
fullness. Stretching from energetic roots in Gaia, our mother, to
the portals of celestial wisdom with our star ancestors. We are the

bridge of worlds, the vibration of possibility, the purpose of Love in form.

Make room for the quiet moments.
Make room for the whispers of the fates.
Make room for your heart to breathe into her true essence.
Make room for your wet wings to unfurl and dry in the love of the sun.

The Awakening...

It will look like florescence
A flowering riot of color and shape
The smell of rose, intoxicating
Butterfly pea on my purple lips

It will feel like a becoming
As souls well up to fully inhabit their skins

It cannot be contained

When the air remembers itself as Ha
The breath of our Life
And we shake free of the myth of insignificance

It will smell like the ocean
Wild and free

It will taste of surrender

When the bodies have cleaned themselves
Sacred vessels
Cleared of fear-culture and its dark taint
When life force flows once again with our genius

It will move past the speed of light and the sense of
    sound
into the force that always was
beneath the rubble of forgetting
to be what always was

Love

The Love, power of goddess Gaia in her greenness
Goddess Gaia in her earthly temple of sacred blessings
Emerald planet, a jewel in the universe

And on that day when eyes flutter open to dissolve the
    dreaming,
we will feel the song of the Sidhe
each one a unique note

On that day
    we dream beauty
On that day
    we lose time
On that day
    we sip of eternity
On that day
    that never ends

What would it be like to become honey? To become the slow, sweet nectar of all the hard work that has been done by yourself and your kin. To sit and simmer in that place of restorative rest. To tend the soul's simple desires like sunsets and hugs, warm coffee and slow walks.

Honey is relational and devoted. Requiring the bees' full commitment in a collaborative dance of sunlight, pollen, and wiggles.

What would honey do in the face of change, in the force of this Great Turning?

I think honey would take her time. She would savor the sweetness of everything that gets stuck to her. Relish in the joy that her presence brings.

Honey is healing.

In Costa Rica, the tiny, stingless Mariola bees create a honey that is so healing, you can put a drop in your eyes to improve your vision or heal an infection. Manuka honey heals wounds. Feel that. Honey so potent with healing that it literally helps you to see and to tend your wounds. Honey that helps us heal. How can we become the honey that heals–ourselves, our families, our communities, our culture–with sweet, softening surrender?

Just begin to imagine the genius of Gaia that creates all of this. That she designed a world where the collective sacrifice of bees, in their irresistible attraction to flowers, might be some of the most potent healing salve available.

Becoming honey means releasing the to-do list in order to feel intuition again. Becoming honey means that I don't have to do it all. I just do my part, and surround myself with others who share my values and are doing their part, too.

Becoming honey means that my curiosity, my attraction, my nuggets of passion are my flowers, and I can devote myself to discovering their nectar because the world needs it. The nectar of my curiosity is medicine. The nectar of your curiosity is medicine. Where are your flowers? How can you plant more of them?

The word *sacred* to a fluttering eye morphs into *scared*. In fear we find forgetfulness, tempting to a weary heart. But this is not the sacred warrior way, and our soul knows this. The forgetting can only last so long. Whether the remembrance and surrender comes early or on your last breath, it comes. I once heard a mother who had tragically lost her very young son say to a room of people, "I knew I had to get over this tragedy, I knew I had to find joy again, and eventually be at peace with the loss of my beloved. Why not choose sooner than later." Why not choose sooner rather than later?

How, then, do we become fully human? We love ourselves into the truth of who we are: our flesh bodies, quantum biological miracles of light, vibration, and love. When we alight the love that powers this magic, we become again the beings of peace that we always have been.

Shedding the layers of fear that hold us in beliefs of scarcity and lack, we find the frequency of the miraculous that enables us to speak the language of stars. Our roots are thirsty for the truth-speak of Earth's message.

We long for our mother. We long to feel her unconditional love for our frailty, our heart. In the sacred humility of our aliveness, we allow Earth to experience herself, and she, in return, holds us in grace. Her abundance is magnificent—emerald planet of beauty.

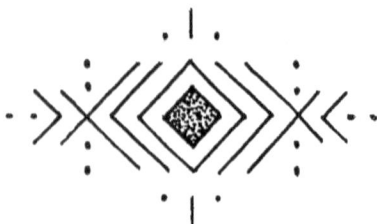

There is no new water on Earth
This water we share
Has been in and through all of us
Connecting the threads of our aliveness
With the aliveness of tree and root
Salt and sand
Only timelines and shape create illusions of difference
Quenching the thirst of parched souls
Washing clean our remembrance...

Feel your roots
Feel your wings
Let them stretch and weave
Let them vibrate with life force

You, too, came by way of starlight. Velocity and white sound pulsed you here, and this is how you have found us, how you have found this page. I am here to re-member you. The wave of light that became you differentiated and embodied so that it could shine in these heavy times. When you feel the weight and density of your body, remember this light. It pulses through your being always and in all ways. Your blessed work in this lifetime is to make way for this light to shine upon the world. So simple. And, within the times of the Turning, not easy.

The secret, hidden truth of these human lives is that we are co-dreaming the world into existence every day. Arriving with a shock into the chaos of earth and cultures of extraction, we exist for a time in a liminal space between star worlds and Earth worlds. And then we begin to thicken. As we thicken, we become increasingly dense and we forget. We forget the power of our dreaming.

Each day, we make the world with our vibratory essence. This essence is supported by our bodies, which are the collaboration of beings that live within us and our interbeing with the fully animate world around us.

Fully animate. All is alive with you.

The truth and power of this dreaming is fed by the resonance of your heart. Your heart, the 12-petaled lotus of ether that arrives with you, complete upon birth, is dimmed as you suffer the traumas of life in a troubled world. This lotus dims until we begin the remembering and begin to give life force to its capacities again. We unfold the 12 petals so the heart can become a fully functioning resonance center again. We remember its power. In this way, we become Love.

The only word we have to describe this miracle of our true being is Love. The love that is the impulse of the universe. The love that is us. You are this. You are starlight, reborn as human. Kin to tree and bird. Kin to water and air. You are this. You are Love.

The spells of the past are flaking off your form to reveal gold hidden beneath. Your life is a ceremony, this planet a temple. You are reborn in every moment. Every moment is a new chance to become. You are never alone.

The cloudy, grey enchantments of a world gone mad fall away, replaced by the sacred drift of our collective geometry, bright and alive with potential. We remember ourselves in alignment with every other being of creation. In this remembering is a deep peace that passes any understanding of the mind. I can love you without ever having met you. I *am* you. We *are* together.

The song of the Sidhe resounds through every cell of my being, and I remember my voice. The unique soul sound that came with me through the clouds of my birth. Thank you for bearing witness to this journey. May it be yours also.

The simple, sacred truth of the world is this:
when we live in the light of our wholesome, whole, and holy Love,
everything we touch, turns to god.

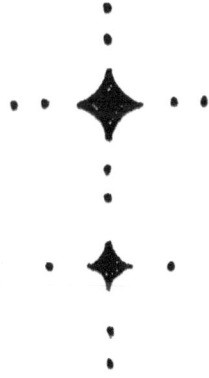

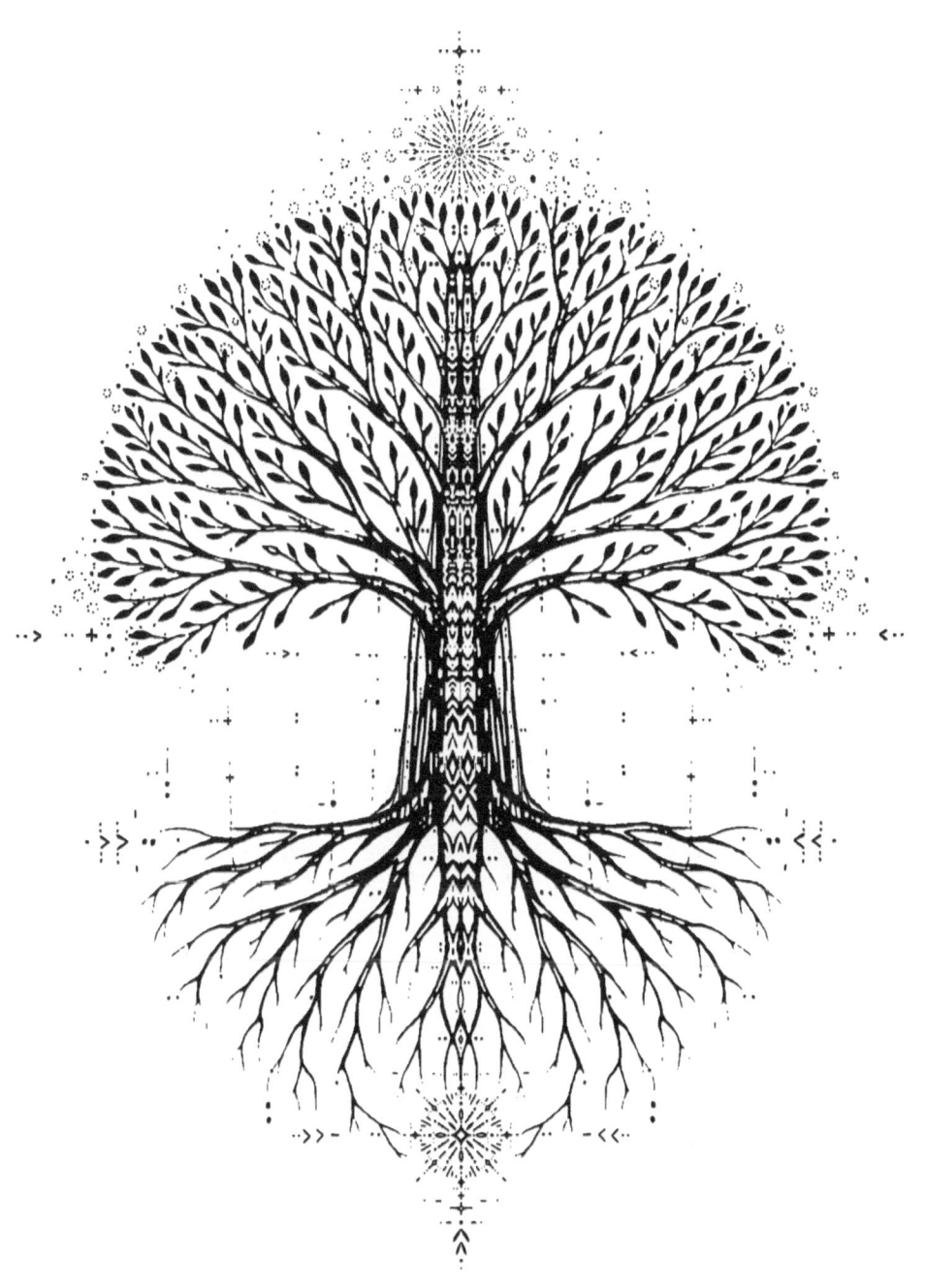

EPILOGUE

A RETURN TO SOIL

'A'ohe pau ka 'ike i ka hālau ho'okahi
All knowledge is not taught in one school

— *HAWAIIAN PROVERB*

From the soils...

At the end of the Turning, when ash becomes thick-
ened, we once again speak soil.

We descend into Earth and breathe our mother through
our pores.

Her deep resonance beating as our heart.

The dirt fills our mouth, and now it is moist with
possibility.

The water and microbes carried in this hummus hum
with new stories of a tomorrow we dreamed before
we forgot, back in the yesterdays of time.

This is the paradox we have danced within.

Unweaving the words so they can whisper in a
language your mind can't hear, that is the way
through.

I once dreamed of waves, taller than the horizon.
Sweeping across the landscape towards me, I was
able to dive down and hold my breath to glide
underneath them.

Below the surface, I found life.

Below the surface, I found you.

When I emerged from the water, there was only soil.

Soil full of seeds.

Seeds full of life.

The codes of our tomorrow are already always within.

May the words of nourishment needed to awaken that
ancient memory be yours.

May you speak them with lilting tones, the tones of
your unique song.

May your heart glow with the possibilities of this
profound peace.

What does it look like for the poet at the end of the
    world?
Drinking of the fresh wild waters
Parched from future dreams
The sacred of silence
The silencing of the sacred
Petals of their whispers, building fungi and fern
Into faerie fort and believing
When wishes meet needs and desires flow
like tides of a portal isle's heartbeat
There is a chance of redemption
We hope not to have to start again
But rather like lichen and vine to wrap our wet,
green tendrils around the dry dying until Life is all
    you see
This is possible, she whispered
Loud in her truth
This is peacemaking
You remember...

She sat on the log
Wet with mourning
And cemented this ancient reckoning

The one that sages spoke of
Cemented it into her becoming...
It is time, she sighed
Time to breathe with the mother once again...

She searched for a page
To hold these thoughts
And landed with lichen
Her braid wet with dew
Holding the crystalline memories of words
Drink for a soul on fire
Drink for a self remembered

And so it is
And so it shall be

A rriving at the crown of spirit, we descend back into Earth to remember her wisdom, our mother, our home. And what now?

What is yours to do? What is ours to do?

How might you become unreasonable in your imagining of beloved futures?

What becomes possible when you fully embrace the immensity of your being, the limitless nature of you as divine and human?

These inquiries and others can animate your days. They can take the place of fear and panic to sow seeds of calm. Sprouting kindness and connection with the human and more-than-human realms. Nurturing your capacity to remain present in the face of mounting pressure and uncertainty.

Imagination is one of the highest human faculties. With imagination, we make worlds and invite miracles. Our thoughts, our ideas, build our physical experiences of reality.

You are already a co-creator of our beloved futures. Lean into this mission. The contraction before birth is the time of most intense pain. On the other side is a love greater than any we have known in this lifetime. Breathe and push, new life is coming.

Contemplation of the possible, seen and understood through the eye of the heart; this is the pathless path to Life-centric futures of interbeing.

To anchor yourself in your own sense of grounded presence, you can begin with simple practices.

Thank your water each day for hydrating your body.

Pause for a moment before you eat to give thanks to your food, the Earth who grew it, and all the hands that prepared it with love.

Breathe.
Stretch.
Hug.

Catch eyes with a stranger and offer your full love to their being.

Notice the world around you in her inestimable beauty and offer her your words of appreciation.
See her.

Notice your peace in the now and guard it with your love for the futures.

As the chaotic uncertainty on the planet increases, become reso-
lute in your search for the others who are awake and aware to our
truth as beings of Earth and peace. We are already many.

ACKNOWLEDGMENTS

I am so grateful to my husband Brady and our children for supporting me in the birthing of this book, creating the conditions of possibility for my life as a writer. To Elen Elenna, author of Sliver Wheel, who held the sacred writing containers and spiral pathways that opened portals... enabling a flood of wisdom and the book's architecture to pour through. Mahalo to Kate Newburgh and Alnoor Ladha for their generous early reading and detailed feedback, reminding me that it is ok to be non-dualistic and paradoxical, that it might be exactly what the world needs right now. Mahalo to artist and illustrator Kris Davidson, who sat in ceremony and allowed the images I had described to him to reveal themselves. To all those who hold me in their hearts and believe in my capacity to share a voice for our beloved temple Earth. Mahalo to Earth herself, sky and ocean. And to all the more-than-human ones who continue to believe in our capacity to remember our place in the dream of the beloved futures. Mahalo ke akua.

ABOUT THE AUTHOR

AUBREY MORGAN YEE, PHD

Aubrey Morgan Yee, PhD is a mythopoetic futurist, author, and facilitator devoted to birthing life-affirming futures through love, remembrance, and sacred action. With a Ph.D. in Alternative Futures and Indigenous Politics, and over a decade of experience in leadership development, Aubrey weaves systems thinking, spiritual ecology, storytelling and Earth wisdom into every space she holds – from global culture labs to moonlit retreats.

As the founder of Our Beloved Futures, steward of Hokuao Farm & Temple, and a mother of two, Aubrey brings grounded vision, poetic insight, and deep presence to all that she offers. She works with seekers, artists, and world builders to awaken possibility and walk with integrity in this era of transformation, known by many as the Great Turning.

Aubrey's work and life is dedicated to remembering what it means to be fully human, to face and metabolize the toxic systems of modernity and to be a luminous guide for those longing to walk a path of peace in service to collective liberation of all beings.

If you want to walk with us at Our Beloved Futures and deepen in the teachings of this book, there are a few steps that you can take.

Join the newsletter and our growing community at **www.ourbelovedfutures.com** to receive information about work-shops, peacemaking circles, inspired writing, and community-building events.

Follow us at **@aubreymorganyee** and **@ourbelovedfutures** for inspiration and connection.

And for those ready to commit in devotion to the deep inner shift towards a purpose-filled life, join me in Chrysalis **www.ourbeloved futures.com/chrysalis**; a journey of personal metamorphosis or Interbeing **www.ourbelovedfutures.com/interbeing**; to cleanse, clear, and align with your soul's most natural form of service in the Great Turning - alongside others walking these pathways of transition.

All are welcome. In your trepidation, your excitement, your fear, your joy, in whatever way your life is unfolding, you are welcome. Compassion, interbeing, and integrity guide our steps. I love you. You are the morning star, rising. We are here.

THANK YOU

REVIEW THIS BOOK

Enjoyed *Our Beloved Futures*? Your feedback means the world! If the book resonated with you, inspired you, or offered something meaningful, we'd truly appreciate it if you left an honest/brief review on Amazon tinyurl.com/bdjshh3x or Goodreads. Your feedback helps others discover the book—and it directly supports the author's work.

About the Publisher

Red Thread Publishing is an award-winning indie press dedicated to amplifying powerful, authentic nonfiction voices. In our first five years, we've published more than 68 books, supported over 320 authors from 30 countries, and celebrated 39 book awards, proof of the impact and quality behind every title we produce.

Our passionate team is committed to guiding authors through every step of the writing and publishing journey so their stories not only get published but make a lasting impact.

Visit **www.redthreadbooks.com**

Email us **info@redthreadbooks.com**

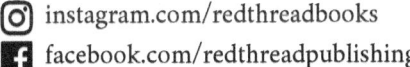 instagram.com/redthreadbooks
facebook.com/redthreadpublishing

NOTES

4. THE DISSOLVING

1. Ladha, Alnoor and Murphy, Lynn. *Post Capitalist Philanthropy: Healing Wealth in the Time of Collapse*. (The merkaba comes from this book).

5. MARIPOSA

1. Bibhu Dev Misra, *"The End of the Kali Yuga in 2025: Unraveling the Mysteries of the Yuga Cycle,"* Graham Hancock (blog), June 2017, https://grahamhancock.com/dmisrab6/.

8. SOLAR PLEXUS

1. Bambara, Toni Cade. 1982. Interview by Kay Bonetti. In Conversations with Toni Cade Bambara, edited by Thabiti Lewis. Published by Johns Hopkins University Press.

9. HEART

1. Stuart, Brooke. 2022. "On the Toroidal Field." *Let Go & Grow* (blog), December 7, 2022. https://www.drbrookestuart.com/on-the-toroidal-field
2. Akomolafe, Bayo. 2022. "The Invisible Constituency of the Slave Ship." Blog post, February 16, 2022. https://www.bayoakomolafe.net/post/the-invisible-constituency-of-the-slave-ship.

www.ingramcontent.com/pod-product-compliance
Lightning Source LLC
Chambersburg PA
CBHW031459120626
46545CB00005B/1680